MANAGING CURRICULUM MATERIALS IN THE ACADEMIC LIBRARY

Alice S. Clark

THE SCARECROW PRESS, INC.
Metuchen, N.J., & London
1982

Library of Congress Cataloging in Publication Data

Clark, Alice S.
    Managing curriculum materials in the academic library.

    Includes index.
    1. Library education--United States. 2. Curriculum
planning--United States. 3. Libraries, University and
college--United States. I. Title.
Z668.C65   027.5'2777   81-16574
ISBN 0-8108-1482-X   AACR2

TABLE OF CONTENTS

ACKNOWLEDGMENT

Much of the material for this book appeared as research in dissertations and other printed sources and is listed in the bibliographic notes. However, special credit is due to Royce P. Flandro, Harlan R. Johnson, Donald S. MacVean and Carol Ruth St. Cyr whose dissertations are extensively quoted and whose fine research deserves a wider exposure. The work of all of these people has documented the basic pattern of service in curriculum materials libraries.

The author is grateful to Rollin George Douma for permission to include his model selection policy for schools and to Urania Gluesing for approving the inclusion of her model pathfinder for use of a curriculum collection.

The author also wishes to acknowledge the contributions made by the curriculum materials librarians whose experience and knowledge helped to define the practices and policies currently used in curriculum collections:

Barbara Biebush, Sonoma State University
Christine Buder, New Mexico State University
Barbara Clarke, State University of New York, Geneseo
Harlow Clarke, Sacramento County Board of Education
Stan Frost, Sacramento State University
Urania Gluesing, San Francisco State University
David Kreh, State University of New York, Cortland
Leora Lucas, State University of New York, Oneonta
Jeryl Mitchell, Syracuse University
Jeff Paul, San Jose State University
Frank Smith, New Mexico State University

Grateful acknowledgment is also due to the staff of the Interlibrary Loan Section of the University of New Mexico General Library for excellent service and to Margaret Weinrod for her patience and assistance in typing the manuscript.

Alice S. Clark

CHAPTER 1

THE CURRICULUM MATERIALS CENTER
AS A SERVICE AGENCY

As early as the 1920s, collections of textbooks and
samples of curriculum guides, research and teaching units,
and lesson plans were set aside in what were called "curriculum laboratories." These collections were developed by the
faculty in colleges and departments of education and used to
teach curriculum planning so that students preparing for a
career in teaching could become familiar with the materials
needed for their future classroom use. These curriculum
laboratories developed into extensive libraries of published
and unpublished materials, production centers where education
students learned to prepare their own materials, and instructional areas where college faculty could introduce students to
the process of developing curriculum for future professional
use.

As the storage and service functions of these curriculum materials centers expanded, problems of management
arose as a result of the difficulties of acquiring a constant
flow of new materials, the extensive work involved in a classification system needed to keep them in order for easy retrieval,
and the need for commitment of ever-increasing resources of
money and personnel by the college or department of education. The very obvious overlap with the functions of the general library of the college or university frequently resulted
in a transfer of the management of the curriculum laboratory
to the library organization.

The purpose of this book is to help the college or university librarian understand and maintain the best of those
functions which were offered when the centers were based in
the college of education, while improving the service through
the application of traditional library procedures. Some of the
information needed to administer a collection of curriculum
materials appears in the literature of curriculum development

1

and educational methods, but much of the best research has
appeared only in the form of dissertations in the field of education. It is hoped that this book will bring together the useful results of existing research in a form which will be more
easily used by practicing librarians and that this will assist
them in offering maximum service to the users of curriculum
materials.

History and Definition of the Curriculum Materials Center

The curriculum laboratory, using that name, started
as a concept in the early twentieth century. Its function was
to create or develop curriculum and it was often called a
"laboratory" because its purpose was research into the construction of curriculum. The first organized center may have
been at Western Michigan in 1922; it was called the Textbook
and Curriculum Service Library.[1] A major influence on the
trend toward developing such collections was the development
of the Curriculum Construction Laboratory which was started
at Columbia Teacher's College in 1924. A study by Leary in
1937 indicated that there were 107 curriculum laboratories in
the United States by that time. Curriculum laboratories were
defined as having "special browsing or work facilities and
special resources for curriculum study."[2]

A wide variety of names have been used over the years
to describe the teaching materials facility. Some of them are:

Curriculum Laboratory
Curriculum Library
Curriculum Center
Curriculum Inquiry Center
Curriculum Materials Center
Curriculum Materials Li-
    brary
Educational Materials Center
Education Resource Center
Education Library
Educational Media Evaluation
    Center
Educational Media Selection
    Center
Instructional Aids Center
Instructional Materials
    Center
Instructional Resource
    Center
Instructional Materials Lab-
    oratory
Instructional Materials Eval-
    uation Center
Instructional Media Selection
    Center
Learning Resources Center
Learning Materials Library
Teaching Materials Center
Teaching Aids Center
Teaching Materials Library
Teaching Aids Library

There are also other variations of the above terms. The

problem of identifying the location of a curriculum materials collection is compounded by the fact that some of these terms are often used also to denote a general library collection or a multimedia collection rather than a center devoted to curriculum materials. For many years the term "curriculum laboratory" was considered the standard terminology but in recent years the wider variety of names has appeared. In this book the term generally used is "curriculum materials center."

While there is a tendency to believe that the public school curriculum of the 19th century consisted of a simple reliance on McGuffey's readers or Noah Webster's blue-backed speller, actually a variety of teaching texts and techniques were in use. Field trips for nature study, educational games, spelling bees, and the drawing of maps and charts of botanical specimens were among the varied teaching methods used. By the 1930s, researchers in the field of education were routinely applying the elements of sociology and psychology to the preparation of a variety of curriculum materials. Under the pressure of commercial competition, publishers were providing sets of textbooks with accompanying manuals and workbooks as well as other reading materials which developed a subject through a planned progression from grade to grade. Often a state department of education or a school district would develop a syllabus which created standards and set the limits of what was to be taught so that some conformity would exist for a number of schools or school districts.

Research in education brought a scholarly examination of the learning process and the study of teaching methods, and curriculum development became part of the course work for students entering the field of elementary and secondary education. The training programs for teachers expanded from a few weeks of preparation to two years, then three years, and eventually became a degree program or a five-year degree-plus practicum course. It soon became evident that as a professional, the teacher would individually develop and revise curriculum, and that both pre-service and in-service teachers needed to be given a place where samples of curriculum materials could be examined and the process of curriculum development learned and practiced. It was the recognition of this need by teaching faculty in colleges and departments of education which brought about the establishment of collections of curriculum materials. By the 1960s greater use of the new nonbook media was stimulated by the National Defense Education Act, Title VII, which supported research, experimentation and dissemination of new media, and audiovisual media were included in the curriculum collections. By this time the location of curriculum centers was changing from the colleges and departments involved in teacher training to the general or education library.

The Primary Role of the Curriculum Materials Center

Curriculum is usually defined as all of the experiences which a student has while in a controlled school environment. Curricula are planned and constructed to provide a multifaceted exposure to such teaching techniques as lectures, reading and audiovisual exercises, observations, laboratory experiments, dramatizations, drill or practice, and testing. The purpose is the transfer of knowledge through the learning of individual concepts which lead to a general understanding of any subject. The development of curriculum is a continuous process of revision for improvement and to reflect changes in trends, principles and practices in the field of education.

Paul Witt, in an article on pre-service education of teachers, said that teachers will not be properly trained if they do not have actual experience with materials. [3] Education students need to study materials by actually examining them, judging them and then using those they select. As a result of this need, the curriculum center is required to provide a wide range of sample materials, equipment for examining and using them, and proper space and facilities for study and practice.

Most of the research on curriculum materials centers describes a more complex set of functions than just the provision of materials. The functions of a curriculum materials laboratory may include all or part of the following activities:

1. To evaluate and select curriculum materials and to teach and assist the clientele in this activity
2. To procure materials and to teach and assist others in locating sources for rental, borrowing, or purchase
3. To catalog and organize materials for retrieval by patrons of the center and to provide the assistance and instruction necessary for retrieval
4. To house and maintain a current collection using proper procedures for safety and preservation

5. To circulate the materials as specified by standard policies
6. To produce materials and to assist and teach the center's users in the production of materials
7. To coordinate services with other agencies so that users of the center have access to all services contributing to curriculum development
8. To serve as an information center for curriculum development by advice and consultation on research, editing and reviewing of materials, publishing data on state and community teaching resources, and conducting any activities which promote the growth of teaching skills.

The most emphasized function was, however, the provision of curriculum materials. As James reported the situation: "The activities and services were primarily those related to providing materials--textbooks and curriculum guides--to pre- and in-service teachers. Very few laboratories were engaged in curriculum improvement workshops or seminars."[4]

The decline in emphasis on curriculum construction met with frequently expressed opposition. Research studies comment on the fact that the emphasis in service to students was on the provision of materials, and they show a prejudice against and a lack of understanding of the teaching role of the reference librarians working in the centers. Many reports indicate that the primary researcher did not see librarians as experts in materials evaluation and information retrieval, elements which are a large part of curriculum development.

The three basic requirements which seem to have prevailed are a place where curriculum construction or revision is done; a collection of materials (published, unpublished and raw materials for construction); and personnel with expertise in giving assistance, direction and guidance to students working on curriculum. MacVean found that users, in order of frequency, were students in methods classes, student teachers, other education students, local teachers, and college faculty.[5]

The first responsibility of the curriculum materials center was, of course, to the students enrolled in the teacher training program of the parent institution, and the functions of the center evolved to meet their needs.

In 1957, a statement, Standards for State Approval of Teacher Education, was prepared as a project by the National Association of State Directors of Teacher Education and Certification with assistance from the U.S. Office of Education. This document was a revision of the USOE Circular No. 351, Proposed Minimum Standards for State Approval of Teacher Preparing Institutions. These standards required both collections and production facilities for all types of media, and named the library as one suitable location for the curriculum laboratory:

> 2.7.5 Curriculum Laboratories. A materials laboratory or center should be maintained either as part of the library or as one or more separate units. It should be open to students as a laboratory of materials of instruction and should be directed by a faculty member well-informed in the various instructional media and materials at different grade levels. This laboratory should include a wide array of books commonly used in elementary and secondary schools; various types of audiovisual aids such as maps, charts, pictures, film-strips, and recordings; various types of materials used in evaluating learning; curricular patterns, courses of study, and teaching units. These should be workshop facilities for preparing new curriculum materials including access to electronic, photographic and other equipment. [6]

The standards do indicate that more than one unit may be involved--allowing for the audiovisual services of the materials production facility to be separate from the collection of sample materials.

The Secondary Role of Serving Local Teachers

Most academic centers which collect teaching materials experience a moderate amount of use by community teachers. This seems to occur even in cases where the school system maintains a good variety of such materials for teachers. This service to teachers is encouraged by academic administrators who are eager to develop good community relations. The clientele of local users is often made up of five groups:

1. Teachers who are graduates or are taking inservice courses in the academic unit and who knew

and used the center as a student and continue to find it useful because of their familiarity with its personnel, collection, and services

2. Cooperating teachers involved in the student teaching program of the college or department of education and who are introduced to the services of the center through student teachers in their classes

3. Teachers in communities where the funding of the school system is inadequate to supply the breadth of teaching aids required for varied methodology in teaching

4. Teachers in communities where a nearby academic institution has been made the location for an evaluation center for state-approved curriculum materials

5. Community teachers where the director of the academic center is actively involved in a public relations program through interaction at professional education association meetings and through a regular program of holding book fairs or publishers' demonstrations of new materials

The National Association of State Directors of Teacher Education and Certification also has standards for the outside relationships of a college of education and recommends close cooperation which, in effect, requires that local teachers should have access to the curriculum center. [7] Russell found the use by teachers to be: 1) service to curriculum committees, 2) providing materials to assist in accreditation self-studies, 3) providing materials for state committees, and 4) service to teachers taking courses in summer school. Russell's conclusions were that use is limited because information on new curricula is not properly disseminated so that all teachers know about them, that teachers are unaware of committee curriculum work, and that the curriculum materials center could be the agency to bring to teachers the information which they want. [8]

In recent decades there would appear, in theory, to be no reason why the academic centers would need to serve the local community. In actual practice, however, they have always seemed to provide some kind of such service. Since 1956, the American Association of School Librarians has maintained that the school media center should be the agency providing this service. In many cases the school or the school district, the state education department, or a federally

financed regional evaluation center has provided the collection
of curriculum materials for local teachers. Some school
districts have received so much funding that they could even
afford to have several well-equipped satellite centers within
a school, each having basic collections of print and nonprint
materials and maintaining all types of visual and audio equipment for classroom use. Recent setbacks in funding for
schools have begun to throw more community service back
upon the academic centers.

After 1960, the concept of the school district instructional materials center became widespread as a result of state
and federal grants. Often this resulted in a network of centers under the leadership of the state education department.
Some of these networks expanded into systems of automated
bibliographic control of curriculum materials and professional
education literature. During this period there appeared such
nationally-important programs as the Educational Research Information Center (ERIC), the National Information Center for
Educational Media (NICEM), the Instructional Materials Center Network for Handicapped Children and Youth, and the
Technology Resource Center under the Vocational Education
Act of 1963. Statewide programs also appeared in such developments as the San Mateo Educational Resources Center
(SMERC) in California and the Boards of Cooperative Educational Services (BOCES) in New York State.

The district centers of state networks were designed
to supplement the holdings and services of school media
centers. Some served also as textbook storage areas and
provided book processing for school media centers, or supplied expensive nonbook materials, audiovisual equipment,
and special education and vocational education materials to
schools. For example, in 1948, the State Education Department in New York organized the BOCES system and centers
were established throughout the state through a system of increased state aid to participating schools. These centers
provided curriculum development services and facilities;
shared teaching personnel for such areas as art, physical
education and school libraries; and took a major role in providing vocational education and education of physically and
mentally handicapped children.

Some of these systems have declined or are in danger
of losing funding. When state funds are cut, school districts
are sometimes reluctant to spend any of their limited funds
for purposes outside of their immediate control. Where there

has been a drop in state or federal funding, a return to greater community dependence on the academic-based curriculum center has occurred.

The college or university curriculum materials center cannot equal those of the best school districts or those of city and county cooperative centers maintained by several schools or districts. Because of the nature of the university clientele, there is much less demand for either variety or quantity of service and materials. The role of the instructional materials center in the academic library is directed more toward providing samples and examples of materials for limited outside use, and the libraries seldom supply any substantial quantity of 16mm film or have much equipment for lending. These centers usually ignore many of the things which a school or district center would supply, such as repair parts and bulbs for equipment, microscope slides, reagents, and biological specimens. The role of the instructional materials center in the academic library is more limited and its library function is its most prominent activity.

One frequent use of the college or university curriculum collection is by school curriculum committees. These groups may schedule several meetings in the curriculum center's conference room at which committee members will review textbook series, do research on curriculum guides or courses of study from other systems or states, and preview audiovisual materials for possible recommendation for purchase. Arrangements may be made for lending a large group of materials to a school for extensive examination and testing in classes.

Relationships with Practicing Teachers

The academic curriculum materials center has an advantage in its service to practicing teachers in that it can provide well-educated personnel advised and supported by the education department faculty working on the experimental fringes of their field. Location in the library has brought the resources of a second university group to the support of the center and has insured that the curriculum materials collection will be served with the latest technology available to library science. When this dual interest of two university departments exists, it has helped to maintain the budget at an adequate level.

A study of the use of the Curriculum Materials Center at the University of Michigan showed that the low use by experienced teachers and administrators was due to their lack of knowledge that the Center existed or to insufficient knowledge of what services it offered. The conclusion was that "The main interest of all the experienced teachers and administrators, those who had used the Center as well as those who had not used the Center, was to make the Center and its available materials known more widely." This group felt that off-campus circulation of the materials was very important. They said they needed to use such a collection for preparation of new curriculum and for getting new ideas for classroom use. [9]

The teacher education faculty usually favors loans to teachers throughout the state since many schools lack the materials that teachers need, and the loans create a better relationship between the college or university and the public schools. However, there are objections to off-campus use of materials, based partly on the philosophy of what makes a laboratory collection most useful and partly on the costs involved in extensive off-campus service. Good service off campus with minimum losses to the collection requires a well-functioning circulation system which enables the library to keep good control of the location and loan periods for all materials and to maintain good borrower identification records. For this reason it is important that the circulation functions of the curriculum materials center operate under the policies of the library's circulation department, with some local flexibility permitted as needed. Loans not made directly to the people coming to the center need to be handled by the library's interlibrary loan service, which can use the best technology for the lending records, has the means for handling shipping duties, and can maintain accounting records where photocopying or other costs are involved. To duplicate such services in the center would make off-campus lending very expensive. Off-campus lending of curriculum materials can be a major function of a learning materials center in the academic setting, but the decision should be based upon the philosophy of the circulation policies of the library as a whole and on how the institution defines a laboratory collection.

Relationships to Other Agencies

If the curriculum materials center is not well supported by the expertise available in other campus institutions such as the computer center, psychology testing center, or campus video services, its service to the campus and community will be limited. All forms of new technology cannot always be available in the center itself. The staff of the learning materials center must be of high quality and be able to take advantage of the expertise of other librarians if the center is to be as active in service as it should be, and to be something more than just a special library collection. The ability to set up interaction with the reference and computer-searching librarians or with special collections and rare materials experts may provide teachers and students with greater access to professional information or to original research materials useful in classroom teaching. Automated searches of the ERIC and NICEM data bases are needed by users who wish to keep abreast of the latest research and media production in their field. Access to copies of local historical photograph collections or local oral history tapes may not be possible in the center, but its personnel should be able to make referrals to other areas of the library where such materials do exist and where copies can be made for classroom use. If the curriculum materials center does not provide production facilities for creating posters, charts, learning centers, or multimedia programs, it must have close interaction with other units on campus that can supply these forms of curriculum materials to the center's clientele.

Supplementary Collections and Services

One fairly recent change in the nature of curriculum materials collections has been the addition of adult and college textbooks and course support materials. Vocational materials needed for programs under the Manpower Development and Training Act, the Vocational Rehabilitation Act and the Economic Opportunity Act are sometimes provided by the curriculum laboratory to support education programs sponsored by the college or university extension department.

The curriculum center has sometimes been seen also as the logical depository for materials used in the college's tutoring centers and developmental educational programs. Because of the overlap with hi-lo (high interest, low reading level) materials which are used in secondary schools, this has been a very satisfactory melding which discourages unnecessary duplication. The only cautionary statements which seem to be expressed by practicing curriculum center per-

sonnel are: 1) that their centers should not be used as textbook storage areas for multiple classroom copies of workbooks and other special items, and 2) that the center should
not take on the additional duty of collection in these areas
without additional resources in budget and space.

Where the academic curriculum materials center becomes a regional media evaluation center under state or district financing, it can double as the selection center for
schools choosing textbooks and other teaching aids and at the
same time supplement other functions of the school or district media centers.

While educational media evaluation centers are not
synonymous with curriculum materials centers in the academic
library setting, in some areas the academic materials center
may be used as a media evaluation center for state-approved
materials. The educational media evaluation center (EMEC)
has been defined as "a place which houses a wide variety of
media and which conducts a full-scale training program in
the techniques of selecting and using media for librarians,
teachers, educational supervisory personnel, and other
adults."[10] Its primary role is to meet the needs of practicing professionals and it is often under the administration
of a school system, a county or state educational department
or a consortium of schools and libraries. Some of the better
EMECs have been developed where a state-adopted textbook
and educational materials program is in effect, and the center acts as a depository for those materials approved for use
in the schools of the state. As a depository, the EMEC becomes the place where teachers and media specialists from
the schools can examine all of the approved materials and
select those they wish to use in their schools. If an academic
curriculum materials center is chosen to be such an evaluation
center, it will have some added advantages:

1. Publishers who wish to have their materials used
    in the state's public schools will deposit samples
    without charge
2. Public school personnel will use the center exten-
    sively and prepare evaluation forms rating the ma-
    terial
3. A close relationship will be developed with the re-
    sponsible agency of the state education department,
    and this will help to keep the curriculum materials
    center personnel cognizant of the state's educational
    developments

4. The curriculum center's director will be viewed as a part of a broader educational team.

The EMEC has, besides its role as a depository, responsibility for a program of instruction in selection and evaluation of media. It will, however, be teaching this function to experienced teachers who are already knowledgeable in the construction of curriculum. As a result its teaching functions, while narrower than those of the curriculum center, will operate at greater depth on the selection and evaluation element. Clearly, the functions of the two types of centers overlap, as do the functions of curriculum development and media selection.

There are other differences in the operations of the two types of centers. Since the EMEC teaches evaluation and selection, it should also provide those professional materials concerned with the theoretical approach to this subject. The curriculum center does not need to house these professional materials since other departments of the library will provide them. The curriculum materials center can concentrate on the more practical aspects of the subject and the application of theory which is taught in the classroom. At the same time its approach can be more theoretical and innovative in some ways because the materials may not be used by the children themselves or, if they are, it will be in a practice teaching or research situation during the short assignment of the student teacher to the class. The product of the evaluation center's functions, on the other hand, directly affects the educational system, and sometimes for a long period, as when a textbook series is adopted and used for five years. In the curriculum materials center there will be more emphasis on testing experimental materials, since the interest of the academic faculty may be in new teaching strategies and experimental learning techniques.

Where the educational media evaluation center and the academic curriculum materials center are similar is in the management of a depository collection and in the instructional program, which has similar needs in facilities, equipment, collections, and services. It is clear that where no evaluation center is provided for teachers by some governmental agency, the academic curriculum materials center serves many of the evaluation center's functions and has a greater responsibility for serving off-campus clientele. Where an evaluation center does exist in a community, the curriculum center can best maximize its own services by maintaining a close liaison with the evaluation center and by setting up a system for referring people to the other center when appropriate.

Some curriculum laboratories, such as the Curriculum Inquiry Center at the University of California, Los Angeles, have been depositories for state-adopted textbooks and include such special materials as bilingual, Black Studies, and remedial education materials. The advantage of acting as an official state evaluation center, besides the savings in costs of materials when publishers are willing to donate materials, is that the record keeping on use and on teachers' evaluations makes the center more aware of the need for constant self-evaluation, and students are aided by involvement in a situation of actual professional service. Most states require reports on activity and collect information which helps to evaluate the textbook selection procedures. Undoubtedly, part of the reason why some states set up textbook commissions to adopt materials for the public schools was a belief that local selectors lacked the ability to make good selections. Even if this assumption is not true, the advantage of access to the opinions of a broader group of people cannot help but improve the selection process.

Janice Gallinger, in a paper commenting on the proposed national system of educational media selection centers, described in the Guide to the Development of Educational Media Selection Centers, described the relationship of those centers to the academic curriculum center:

> On these campuses there must be an educational media selection center, really the curriculum laboratory expanded, which serves the needs of persons who expect to teach and those who are teaching them how to become teachers. The institution should not rely on centers serving area schools but the two centers should be complementary, each with its own purpose. The needs of college faculty and students are too immediate and demands too heavy to make it practical for them to be served except locally in house.

It was her opinion that colleges and universities should be the leaders in evaluation and selection, not the followers of public schools.[11]

The Trend to the Library-Administered Curriculum Center

The role of the curriculum materials center in an institution of higher learning was seen by Flandro as differing
from that of the school or school district center in that it
served a wider community, supported the teacher preparation
courses, and dealt with the broader problems on a theoretical
basis. [12] The emphasis on acquiring, storing, servicing, and
cataloging materials was the basis for the move of curriculum
centers from the colleges and departments of education to the
academic library. The library had traditionally been a campus agency which served a wider community. Eleanor Ellis
reported in 1969 that 56 percent of the centers in 303 re-
sponding institutions were in colleges of education and 37 percent in libraries, showing a trend which has continued toward
placing the curriculum materials center within the library organization. [13] Betty Jean Houlihan, in an article published in
December 1978, stated that while there was debate about the
administration of the center, "The University Library seems
to predominate in current professional thinking. "[14]

The reasons usually given for the move include a lack
of sufficient personnel and budget, probably because the function was too far removed in the organization from the administration responsible for its budget. An inadequate budget
sometimes meant that service was provided by clerical personnel supervised only part-time by an education faculty member. Centers ended up with a wide variety of personnel and
this sometimes resulted in a caretaker-type of operation. [15]
Another major problem was the need for personnel trained
in organizational theory. More service could be provided if
a unit already set up for processing through acquisitions and
cataloging was available for such work. Remoteness from the
administration often resulted in a failure to realize the space
problems as the collection and services grew and developed.
An agency whose major goal was classroom teaching and
which often had too few classrooms for its own needs was
reluctant to give up additional space for this support function.
All too often, if space was available, it did not meet the requirements of materials storage which are common in library
buildings--high load capacity of floors, adequate protection
from heat and humidity, and security systems for protection
from theft.

Even when a professional librarian was in charge, the
lack of interaction with library faculty peers and the lack of
access to the more modern but expensive library facilities

often hampered the professional growth of the individual. As
new innovations such as OCLC cataloging, automated circulation systems, and online searching service became general
tools in the academic library setting, the isolation of a curriculum collection from the general library's information
systems became a more acute problem.

Another disadvantage of the education department as
a setting for the curriculum collection was the limited opening
hours, often necessary in a classroom building. Many classroom buildings closed at six or nine p.m. and few were open
the long hours provided in a library building. Limited personnel available to keep such buildings open resulted in
shorter hours of service and in some cases increased the
need for duplication of certain curriculum materials in the
library, where they could be used in the late evening hours
and on weekends. These conditions encouraged a change in
the location and administration of the curriculum materials
center from the education department to the general library.

Education administrators often felt that the best and
newest equipment must be committed to classroom use by
their faculty, and thus put the equipment needs of the curriculum support center lower on their priority list. While
they wanted and saw the need for the supporting service of
the curriculum materials center, their decisions were based
on the college's primary function of classroom teaching.

A major problem associated with any collection of
materials is the technical processing function. The processes of acquisition, classification, cataloging, marking and
serials control soon overwhelmed the personnel in many curriculum materials centers, to the detriment of reference and
teaching service. A wide variety of classification schemes
led to further problems. Modifications of the Dewey Decimal
Classification or the Education Laboratory Scheme put out by
the U.S. Office of Education were widely used. Unfortunately, the modifications were often made without a thorough understanding of classification theory and all the ramifications
of the changes made. As a result these schemes quickly
broke down as more complicated combinations and applica-
tions became necessary for new bibliographic and physical
forms of material.

There are, of course, good reasons why the library is
not always the best place for the curriculum collections.
While the curtailment of what was in many areas a duplica-

tion of services seems desirable, problems can arise if the librarian who manages the collection does not have a background in the field of education, does not interact enough with the faculty teaching curriculum and methods courses, and is not committed to the needs of these special library users. The curriculum materials center was meant to be actively involved in providing the means for the development of curriculum, but this may not always be a direct or primary goal of the library-centered collection. It should be understood that the primary purpose is to aid in curriculum development by providing published teaching aids, a collection of ideal examples of lesson plans, teaching units, courses of study, and curriculum guides, and a commitment to provide reference service and advice to those education students and community teachers who are developing curriculum. Without the active advice and involvement of the faculty teaching in the field of education, the collection and its servicing will not fulfill the primary goal.

Curriculum materials cannot be organized on the shelves in quite the same way as general monographic and periodical collections of the library are handled. Their arrangement for browsing and service requires a set of criteria which differs from the emphasis on subject and author involved in handling other library materials. The curriculum materials center becomes a special library within the general library system regardless of its location; its identity and arrangement include recognition of the importance of grade levels, readability levels, the currency and short life of the materials, emphasis on ephemeral and self-produced materials, and the importance of the publisher rather than the individual author in many educational materials. These characteristics, plus the laboratory role of a curriculum materials center, make it appropriate to maintain the center as a separate subset of the general library collection.

One difficulty which has arisen in placing the curriculum collection under the library's administration is the tendency of some administrators to expect the center's personnel to collect and manage all library audiovisual services--especially where the college-level media services to individuals are fairly limited. This practice can weaken the primary function if the budget for materials and personnel is not proportionately increased.

Another disadvantage of the library as the administrative unit for the curriculum materials center is the fact that

doing it better is expensive. Appropriately trained personnel
can be an expensive item. Any duplication in service is
therefore to be avoided. The most desirable situation calls
for a melding of service to college of education faculty and
students by all librarians involved in handling the literature
of the education field. This allows a cooperative approach
to collection development, minimal duplication, and fewer
conflicts in deciding what should be in the curriculum collection and what in the professional education or reference collection. Before the purchase of expensive sets is made, the
possible use in all areas can be surveyed and plans made for
referring all future users to the correct location. People
from the various locations can become familiar with the total
education collections. Difficulties are sure to arise about
where reference books or periodicals are to be located, but
a commitment by each of the persons who have responsibility
in the field will help them see the total picture. Even the
cataloger responsible for classification and descriptive cataloging of curriculum materials will be aided by being part of
the support team handling the professional education materials.
Knowledge of new trends in education and their effect on curriculum materials in elementary and secondary education will
enable the cataloger to anticipate new subject headings and
relationships between subjects and to make careful decisions.

There are good philosophical reasons why the library
should be the administrative location for the curriculum center. By definition schools have been given the role of teaching the body of knowledge, while the more limited support
function of organizing, storing and teaching the way to find
such knowledge in recorded form is the function of the library. For this reason the handling of curriculum materials
belongs more properly in the library than in a teaching department. The materials collection is a support service to
the teaching function of the education faculty, helping education students and community teachers become aware of the
options available to them in a wide variety of recorded forms
from an almost unlimited number of authors, producers, publishers, and other sources. As a result of exposure to this
variety of styles, content, and form, future teachers will be
able to meet the different needs found in individuals, grade
levels, and ability groupings, and to offer the special resources which are available for enrichment, developmental,
and ungraded education. While the variety of sources for
the materials will be a problem, this type of library service
can lead to a spirit of creativity which sparks the teacher to
produce for his/her own classroom use a varied and effective
curriculum.

Conclusion

While there is probably no ideal organizational placement for the curriculum materials center, its proper role in the university setting was well described by Theodore Frank Yuhas:

> The basic recommendation for the laboratory's development is that its planning be in harmony with the development of the general university library and research facilities. This outline can be carried on both under departmental advisement and through central administrative organization. The inescapable fact is that, regardless of departmental control, laboratory direction must be in full understanding and close cooperation with these established main university facilities. This makes it possible for the laboratory to maintain at all times a complementary, rather than competitive, role in the instructional program of the university. There is danger to the laboratory in its developmental years lest its acquisitions parallel those of other existing facilities largely because of the simple expedient of convenience. The laboratory can best acquire stature through its own unique developmental plan where its particular function is being constantly examined to determine how close its purpose is being met.
> As already stated the function of the laboratory is the study of the curriculum.[16]

NOTES

[1]Nevil, Leota, "A Survey of Curriculum Laboratories in Selected Colleges in Pennsylvania" (Master's Thesis, Wilkes College, 1975), p. 13.

[2]Ibid., p. 15.

[3]Paul W. Witt. "Preservice Education in the Selection and Use of All Types of Instructional Materials with Implications for the School Library," in The School Library as a Materials Center, ed. Mary Helen Mahar (Washington, D.C.: Government Printing Office, 1963), p. 46.

[4]Marian Lucia James, "The Curriculum Laboratory in Teacher Institutions: Its Essential Characteristics" (Doctoral Dissertation, University of Connecticut, 1964), p. 119.

[5]Donald S. MacVean, "A Study of Curriculum Laboratories in Midwestern Teacher Training Institutions" (Doctoral Dissertation, University of Michigan, 1958), p. 48.

[6]National Association of State Directors of Teacher Education and Certification. Standards for State Approval of Teacher Education, 4th ed. (Salt Lake City: National Association of State Directors of Teacher Education and Certification, 1971), p. 15.

[7]Ibid., pp. 15-16.

[8]Thomas Edward Russell, "Selected Implications for College and University Curriculum Laboratories in Supporting Public School Curriculum Development" (Doctoral Dissertation, University of Alabama, 1966), pp. 121-123.

[9]Carol Ruth St. Cyr, "Present and Potential Uses of the University of Michigan Curriculum Materials Center" (Doctoral Dissertation, University of Michigan, 1955), p. 57.

[10]John Rowell and M. Ann Heidbreder, Educational Media Selection Centers (Chicago: American Library Association, 1971), pp. 1-2.

[11]Janice Gallinger, "Education Media Selection Centers and Academic Libraries," paper presented at the annual meeting of the American Library Association, New York, N.Y., 1974, p. 3 (ED 095 838).

[12]Royce P. Flandro, "Curriculum Laboratories in Colleges of Teacher Education" (Doctoral Dissertation, Indiana University, 1957), p. 57.

[13]Eleanor V. Ellis, The Role of the Curriculum Laboratory in the Preparation of Quality Teachers (Tallahassee, Florida: Florida A. & M. Foundation, Inc., 1969), p. 47.

[14]Bettyjean Houlihan, "The University Curriculum Library: Evaluate, Update, Renovate," Curriculum Review 17 (December, 1978): 363.

[15] Ellis, The Role of the Curriculum Laboratory, p. 50.

[16] T. F. Yuhas, "The Curriculum Laboratory in the University," Educational Administration and Supervision 38 (April, 1952): 241.

CHAPTER 2

ADMINISTRATION

The Center as a Unit of Larger Systems

    As defined by several researchers, the requirements
for the process of curriculum development might be dia-
grammed as follows:

                    Curriculum Development

Materials	Personnel	Space	Equipment
Selection	Director	Storage	Storage
Acquisition	Professional staff	Display	Repair
Organization	Support staff	Study	Service
Production	Student aides	Small group	Use
Retrieval		Large group	
		Workroom	
		Service	
		Office	

    In meeting these requirements good administration and man-
agement play an important part. Good management principles
should be applied in order to bring together the elements
which will meet the desired objectives of the program. Formal policies and procedures must be established, leadership
provided in the development of the program and the supervision of personnel, and responsible control exercised in the
use of resources. One of the requirements for good management is to find the proper role of the center in the organization of the general library and in the college or university.

    As part of a larger system, the curriculum materials
center may share any of its major administrative components:

1. Governance
2. Budget and planning
3. Services
4. Collections
5. Personnel
6. Facilities.

In the academic setting, the administration of the curriculum materials center may be rather complex if its functions are scattered physically in different locations and the responsibility for its services is assigned to several different agencies. In visiting such centers, the user may have to go to one, two, or several places. Since there is good reason not to duplicate facilities, a curriculum center may be designed to include only certain limited functions, but total service will necessitate all of the above components, either supplied in the center or through contracts with another campus agency. It is possible to think of a curriculum materials program as a system rather than as one unit. Under such circumstances, the role of the academic librarian involved in the curriculum materials program should include the integration of good referral services so that the primary clientele of education students and practicing teachers can have access to all of the important functions.

Alternative Organizational Structures

The National Council for the Accreditation of Teacher Education (NCATE) has established guidelines for evaluating professional education programs. These recognize that a center for providing teaching materials may have its administrative location in any one of several university units. The Standards for the Accreditation of Teacher Education include the statement that "A materials and instructional media center for teacher education is maintained either as a part of the library, or as one or more separate units, and supports the teacher education program."[1] This clearly recognizes that the support facility can exist in more than one place in the university. The suggested interpretive questions which accompany the Standards indicate that the center must have materials which "Illustrate the wide array of available instructional media (such as films, filmstrips, realia, audiovisual tapes, transparencies, teaching machines, and closed circuit TV)."[2] The Standards seem to imply that the curriculum materials center may be a system and not necessarily just one unit.

While originally the curriculum laboratory was usually located within the college or department of education, Flandro found centers "integrated primarily with the library, the instructional department, the audio-visual center, and occasionally the research center."[3] As the support for teacher training programs became more complex, an informal system often developed among these areas.

A description of the network of curriculum services at San Jose State College in 1957 showed a typical system:

> At the present time on the San Jose State College Campus, the following laboratory facilities now contribute to the program of teacher education: an audio-visual service center for which new quarters are being built; a kindergarten laboratory-classroom; an industrial arts activity room; an art education workshop; laboratory room with a new science building for science education; a recordings division in the Humanities Room of the Library; and the curriculum planning facilities and instructional materials in the Education wing of the Library.[4]

The San Jose State University system is now better coordinated, with the curriculum materials included in the Library's Media Services Department, and the Library itself no longer has separate subject areas. Audiovisual media and equipment for individual use, the Library's pamphlet collection, and the collection of art prints are now together. In the planned new facilities, video service will be added. At the same time, other facilities support or duplicate the services of the Library curriculum collection.

The traditional administrative arrangement, still used in some institutions, has an organizational chart somewhat like this:

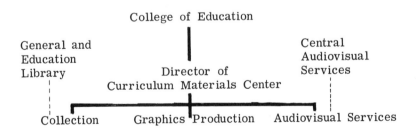

College of Education

General and Education Library

Director of Curriculum Materials Center

Central Audiovisual Services

Collection   Graphics Production   Audiovisual Services

This organizational plan under the college or department of education often keeps the three functions of library, graphics production, and audiovisual production and services separated; a different member of the education faculty takes a leading role in the unit supporting his or her own particular teaching area. The advantage of this organization is that a person with the appropriate technical expertise is extensively involved in direct interaction with students as well as in the management of the unit. In this kind of organizational structure, the main duplication occurs in the collection, the library usually having many of the published items that are in the curriculum center. Where duplication has been carefully avoided, many of the materials which are needed to support the activities of the curriculum center are actually located in the library.

Sometimes a curriculum materials center is organized as a relatively independent unit:

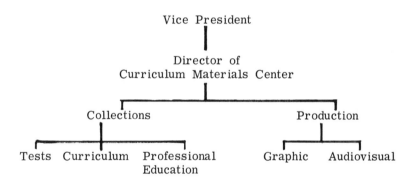

In this system the center provides a relatively complete collection, including tests, and a production unit which supplies all audiovisual and graphic services. Its relationship to general campus services is minimal; it may be linked only to computer services on the university's main frame computer or to a university-supported public television station telecasting to public school classrooms.

A not too untypical organization chart for curriculum services might look like this:

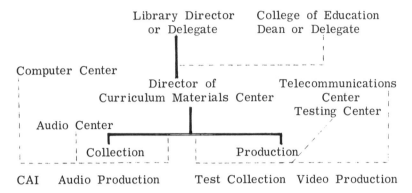

CAI   Audio Production   Test Collection   Video Production

In this system the curriculum materials center provides the curriculum materials but is supplemented by professional education materials in the general library and a complete test collection in a testing center under the education or psychology departments. The production workshop in the curriculum center is self-sufficient for most of the needs of its primary clientele and can provide all kinds of graphic production and facilities and equipment for audio or visual recording, but the services of the university audio center and the telecommunications department provide the more sophisticated services by remote access or referral. Computer-assisted instruction (CAI) is also obtained by remote access to the university's computer services.

While all of these services can greatly contribute to the development of curriculum, the lack of direct administrative governance puts a burden on the curriculum center director to integrate and provide a focus for many diverse contributors. In a realistic situation, a number of artificial constraints may restrict full cooperative service. The curriculum center director may have to accept temporary restrictions, map out a strategy for removing obstacles, and work toward a goal of effective cooperation. The curriculum materials center's relationships on campus are often decided on the basis of expediency or for the purpose of reducing duplication of materials and services. Where the curriculum materials center does not include graphic or audiovisual production facilities, the reason in many cases is that good facilities of this type exist elsewhere on campus and should not be duplicated.

Step one in setting up a coordinated system may be to

identify the lines of authority and to study the nature of the functions of each of the components. It is important to isolate those functions which overlap. This analysis should include the answers to the following questions:

1. Which of the supporting agencies on campus or in the community provide services which are the same as, or similar to, the functions of a curriculum materials center?
2. Who administers each agency?
3. Who provides multimedia services for the agency?
4. Who sets policies and procedures for the agency?
5. What professional services are available at the agency and what expertise does its personnel have?
6. What are its service policies?
7. What media collections does it have?
8. Are materials cataloged and, if so, are they included in the general library's card catalog or automated circulation base?

Such information may improve the possibility of working with the other agencies toward avoiding duplication in materials and services and improving cooperation in the provision of services. Unfortunately, duplication may still be necessary, particularly if an agency has been designed to serve only a special population. The collections in each unit should be examined. Where there appear to be good reasons to duplicate some materials because of differences in clientele and conditions for using materials, compromises may be necessary. The curriculum center may wish to give up its 16mm film collection to the campus audiovisual center because the campus service has better viewing equipment and facilities. On the other hand, the campus audiovisual center, if it has limited use, may be glad to have its filmstrip collection transferred to the curriculum materials center.

While it is unlikely that personnel can be shared on a regular basis, it may be possible to share expertise through advice and consultation. Librarians may be able to offer consultation on organizing materials in other units; equipment experts in other units may offer workshops for library personnel on minor repairs or the use of new technology.

Awareness of mutual concerns and related services may be helpful in persuading directors of the diverse units on campus of the disadvantages of scattered facilities. Cooperative efforts may provide better cable connections for video, audio and computer services. Plans for building future facilities can be improved through recognition of the desirability of good traffic patterns among the related services. Budgeting and planning will always be a reflection of the governance of the units in the system, but a philosophy of cooperation will assist in efficient planning for expansion of services. If budget constraints force a contraction of services, the spirit of cooperation may be even more important, in reducing duplication and making sensible choices as to which services each unit will offer.

Whatever its formal administrative lines and its relationships to other agencies, the curriculum materials center should be a cooperative venture of the library and the college or department of education. It should be located so that there is ready access for maximum traffic from both of these agencies, and it should be staffed by a professional librarian with curriculum training and education.

The Advisory Committee

An advisory committee is one means whereby the curriculum materials center can best meet the needs of its users and take maximum advantage of its role in a cooperative system of support services for education students and faculty. The committee should be made up of representatives from the library, faculty from the department or college of education, and advisors from other cooperating agencies. Representatives from the library might include the supervisor of the center's director, media specialists, the cataloger of the curriculum materials collection, and the bibliographer for professional education materials. Advice from the teacher education faculty can provide direction for meeting changes in the needs of the field; committee members might come from elementary education, secondary education, adult education, the director of field service, the director of student teaching, curriculum or methods courses instructors, or the director of audiovisual and other production services. A strong input from the teacher education faculty is a requirement of the NCATE Standards for the Accreditation of Teacher Education. Interpretive statements in the Standards include: "In maintaining and developing the collection of such materials and media, the institution gives serious consideration to the recommendations of faculty members."[5] Representatives from other supporting agencies can provide the specialized expertise needed to keep the center abreast of new developments in technology. Flandro found that the "most common group found on the steering committees were representatives from the library."[6]

The functions of the advisory committee could include:

1. Advising and approving service policies
2. Advising on the role of the director
3. Assisting in the selection of the director and other professional personnel
4. Advising on the selection policy of the center
5. Advising and approving changes in location, space, and facilities
6. Advising on changes in administrative structure
7. Advising on and supporting budget requests.

While advice on general policies of the center should come from a variety of sources, available via the advisory committee, decisions and the responsibility for them should rest upon the director of the library and his or her delegates, including the director of the curriculum materials center. Because this is the official line of organization, with the responsibility for choosing personnel and allocating the budget, authority and responsibility must be placed there. In order to assure that the curriculum center operates properly in the library setting, the ultimate decisions on policy, selection of the collection, the allocation of the budget, the appointment, promotion or termination of personnel, and the procedures for operating the center must rest with the library administration.

The advisory committee should be involved in the preparation and approval of some of the administrative documents needed to run the curriculum materials center. These would include such statements as:

1. Collection development policies, including gifts and deposits from publishers and individuals
2. Circulation policies, including loan periods, fines, interlibrary loans and lending of equipment
3. Contracts and agreements with the state education department or with school systems
4. Job descriptions for professional personnel
5. Plans for changes in space or location

6. Policy statements on duplication, withdrawals and transfers of the collection
7. Agreements on referrals and cooperation with other campus and community agencies
8. Plans for sponsoring workshops and conferences.

The creation of such documents with the aid of the advisory committee provides the general direction under which the center is administered and the guidance under which the library personnel can act for maximum support of the teacher education program.

The Director and the Professional Staff

When the director of the curriculum materials collection is a member of the general library staff, it may be easier to foster a cooperative campus system. If a tactful and non-threatening approach is used, a librarian may be most effective in developing cooperation because of the library's normal role of addressing the various needs of the whole campus in an impartial manner; it is thus seen as a supporting rather than a competitive service. The library's role in seeking cooperation may be seen as a function of its normal use of referrals for maximum service.

One of the reasons for the trend toward moving the administration of the curriculum collection to the library is the nature of the education and talents needed in a director. Both the education and on-the-job experience of librarians tends to provide some of the most important requirements needed: a broad education, leadership talent, managerial knowledge, selection experience, knowledge of the book trade, and knowledge of classification and cataloging.

It is especially important that the library-based curriculum center director have other attributes which come from a somewhat different background of education and experience. The person preparing for this specialized library service needs to have a knowledge of the field of professional education and familiarity with the needs of children, including those who require bilingual education, special education, or who may have physical conditions that limit their learning progress. The director needs to understand the methods of elementary and secondary teaching and have a knowledge of curriculum development. While not all curriculum centers include responsibility for audiovisual and graphics production,

knowledge of production materials and equipment is still
necessary if the center is to make proper referrals to other
agencies or provide good assistance on guides and manuals
for production service.

John G. Church developed a checklist as part of his
dissertation which can be used for evaluating curriculum materials centers. Included were some of the desirable characteristics which a center's director should possess: three
years of successful teaching experience, experience in curriculum construction and revision, membership in professional
associations relevant to the curriculum center's functions,
graduate work in curriculum, and a doctorate in the field of
education. Church also said that library education, perhaps
at the graduate level, was necessary. [7] While all of these
characteristics are desirable, a combination of some of these
skills and experience from fields of education and library
science are the usual rule.

Another opinion calls for a director who is an expert
in one field and familiar with the other. This, of course,
presupposes that it is not possible to have two professional
positions, each with a specified area of expertise. Unless
the organizational, service, and administrative skills of libra-
rianship are supplemented with a knowledge of the field of
education, there is danger that the center will become just a
library or a library media center. [8]

Church's model of a director does include the expec-
tation that he or she will have the technical expertise of a
librarian. This includes education and experience in selecting, organizing, and using print and nonprint materials. It
implies that the professional staff will know the principles and
procedures of technical processing. Actually only a general
and theoretical knowledge may be necessary, since in the academic library setting these functions can best be performed
by the technical processing departments. The major requirement is for a knowledge of the selection tools and sources
for teaching materials, and the ability to analyze and select
a classification scheme appropriate for several types of collections.

Given a background of training and experience in the
field of education, the curriculum center professional will be
qualified to teach an occasional course in curriculum or
methods and is more likely to be involved in the committees
and other activities of the faculty in teacher education. The

director and professional staff should, however, hold faculty status in the library rather than in the college or department of education, since that is their official administrative structure.

The requirements for serving the needs of the patron directly in reference service and retrieval of information for curriculum development and revision will come from both backgrounds. The need for a professional staff of more than one person is evident, although this may have to be achieved in some cases through part-time assignments from other areas of the library staff. Needed professional expertise requires a curriculum generalist, an education librarian, an administrator, a media production specialist, and a specialist in instructional technology. Because such a variety of specializations is needed, some curriculum materials centers are organizationally located in the reference department of the library, although physically separated. At San Jose State University, the unit is part of Media Services, which in turn is a part of reference and information services. At both San Francisco State University and the University of New Mexico, the curriculum librarian actually serves on the main reference desk and participates in on-line search activities. Even though the curriculum materials center professionals are considered to be assigned full-time to the center, they have brief but regular service assignments to general reference. This has been found to be effective in establishing a liaison which helps curriculum center people learn what tools are available in the reference department to help their students, while they in turn can keep general reference librarians in touch with what is available in the curriculum center. It would seem appropriate that at least some reference librarians serve a similar short work assignment in the curriculum materials center.

Most curriculum librarians do feel that the unit should be a department of the library, since this enables the director to interact with departments other than reference. In this way the center can better integrate its services with government publications collections, media services, circulation services, and the special collections departments. The tendency for center policies to vary widely from those of the rest of the library is probably the result of a communication gap and isolation from other departments.

The duties of the director as a manager include:

1. Planning and administering the program for the curriculum materials center in coordination with the library administration and an advisory body including the teacher education faculty
2. Coordination and liaison with other agencies offering related services
3. Participating in committees and activities of both the library and the college or department of education on matters relating to curriculum development in public and private schools
4. Coordination with the state education department on evaluation and selection of textbooks and instructional materials
5. Conducting public relations activities designed to reach local schools and libraries
6. Serving as chairperson of the advisory committee
7. Taking the major role in the selection, training, and evaluation of the staff of the center
8. Assisting in development of policies
9. Implementing policies with approval of the library administration and the advisory committee
10. Taking responsibility for the conduct of the services and functions of the center, analyzing and solving problems, and applying good management techniques in the running of the center
11. Teaching students, faculty, and others how to make good use of the center, and providing reference and information services
12. Developing budget requests
13. Making internal budget allocations
14. Providing a climate of service to the clientele
15. Keeping statistics and writing reports to the library administration, the advisory committee, and other cooperating agencies as necessary.

Some of the specific tasks of the director would be:

1. To read reviews, evaluate, and select published teaching aids in all forms
2. To do ongoing research on new developments in curriculum revision and on the practices of other instructional materials centers
3. To attend conferences and meetings of the library and the teacher education departments for proper liaison

4. To initiate policies and procedures
5. To train and direct staff
6. To keep records on expenditures which will assure compliance with a planned budget
7. To select equipment for purchase
8. To provide reference service
9. To prepare a user orientation and instruction program
10. To evaluate the curriculum collection on a continual basis and approve withdrawals
11. To conduct user satisfaction studies and make changes where appropriate
12. To write proposals for additional funding
13. To write proposals for program changes for consideration by administrators and the advisory committee.

While Flandro found that most of the professional services in curriculum materials centers were supplied by the director, [9] other professional staff should be chosen to supplement the skills of the director, their professional status to be determined by the education and training they have received in a specialized area. In the university setting this implies at least a master's degree in a suitable field as a requirement. Expertise might be in media or graphics production, instructional television, library technical processing, or instructional technology.

The tasks of the other professional staff should include some of the same tasks that the director of the center would perform. Their duties might include the following:

1. To read reviews and assist in media selection
2. To provide reference and instruction in use of the collection
3. To participate in a user education program
4. To do ongoing research on new developments in curriculum and in management of curriculum collections
5. To teach and direct students in the production of graphic displays, learning centers, puppets, and other three-dimensional teaching aids
6. To teach and direct students in the production of audiovisual media
7. To secure media for preview
8. To seek sources of free materials
9. To produce bibliographies and other publications

useful to the clientele
10. To place orders for new material (if acquisition is a function of the center)
11. To classify and catalog materials (if technical processing is done in the center)
12. To assist in direction of staff and student aides
13. To set up media preview meetings.

The decision on whether or not there should be more than one professional in the curriculum center would appear to be governed by the following factors:

1. Is technical processing of materials done in the center?
2. Will graphic production be done in the center?
3. Will multimedia production take place in the center?
4. Is the volume of use of the center unusually high?
5. Is the director assigned to the center only on a part-time basis?

Support Staff

The Guidelines for evaluation centers call for minimum personnel in even the smallest centers to include: two full time professionals, the director and a media specialist; one general media assistant; one media technician; one administrative assistant; three clerk typists; and one custodian.[10] Among curriculum centers in academic libraries this kind of staffing exists only in very well-supported full-service centers. Custodial service is, however, not included since colleges and universities provide this in other ways. Somewhat less staff is needed if technical processing is done elsewhere, and the extent of audiovisual media service determines the staff needed in that area. A realistic minimal staffing pattern might be:

With Production Services: two professionals--one education librarian and one media librarian, either one acting as director in addition to specialist duties; two general subprofessional assistants with administrative and media assistant duties; two clerical assistants, and student assistants for shelving, desk work, etc.

<u>Without</u> Production Services: one professional education librarian with some background or education in media production and service; one subprofessional assistant with both administrative and media assistant duties; two clerical assistants and student assistants for shelving, desk work, etc.

A minimum of four full-time staff is needed if the normal long hours of the main library are to be maintained. It is certainly not desirable to limit staffing to the point where the center has to maintain shorter hours of service than other library service areas.

If no professional staff other than the director is available, a subprofessional with teaching education or experience should be employed so that reasonable hours of good reference service may be maintained. If this person is the only full-time support staff, it is important that the position be at the subprofessional level so that duties can include advice and instruction to students, demonstration of equipment, and orientation tours, as well as such duties as maintaining files, processing tests, pamphlets, and pictures, and supervision of part-time staff, student assistants, etc.

Other support staff, including student assistants, should be responsible for duties such as the following:

1. Performing circulation functions
2. Processing materials for special reserve
3. Staffing the circulation desk
4. General clerical and stenographic duties
5. Shelving books
6. Reading shelves
7. Checking in new material
8. Arranging displays and bulletin boards
9. Providing basic reference service
10. Preparing materials for filing
11. Repairing materials
12. Filing.

The Budget

In his study of curriculum materials centers, Flandro concluded that "The three primary deterrents to the use of the curriculum laboratory were inadequacies in materials, facilities, and personnel."[11] Clearly, the commitment of an adequate budget is necessary for a successful operation. John G. Church recommended in 1964 that "One of the first objectives of a person desiring to establish a curriculum laboratory is to obtain an item in the budget labelled 'curriculum laboratory'."[12] In the past curriculum centers often did not appear as line items in the budgets of colleges and universities. This reflected the fact that many centers relied primarily on free materials and had only part-time personnel whose first duty was to another area. This kind of loose arrangement is not good management practice, but there are still some institutions where the cost of operating the center is buried in the overall library budget. Often no separate budget is designated for curriculum materials; they may be included as part of a line for education or for audiovisual materials. Items included in serials, or on standing order or approval plans, or in deposits of government publications are often part of the library budget and are not specifically identified as part of the curriculum center budget. If the cost of the curriculum materials center is to be accurately identified and good fiscal management practiced, budget items should be specifically designated:

1. Materials
   Monographs
   Serials
   Standing Orders
   Government publications
   Audiovisual materials
2. Professional personnel
3. Support personnel
4. Student assistants
5. Equipment
6. Supplies and services
7. Travel.

Unless there is such documentation, administrators may well fail to recognize the actual cost of this service; reasonable decisions on increasing or decreasing funds dedicated to the center's collection become difficult or impossible in such circumstances. While accounting in detail of all curriculum center expenditures may not be totally separated from the record of other library costs, it is important that the director of the center and the advisory committee review the budget committed to the center's functions each year and have a good grasp of the actual costs of the operation.

Stull and Holley found in 1960 that "the well-staffed

center with adequate funds of its own was not predominant in the 14 institutions in this study."[13] Curriculum materials librarians still, twenty years later, characterize their units as the "stepchild" of the library. That does not mean that many of them are not well supported. Some, indeed, have space, personnel, and funds allocated almost more generously than the teacher education program would indicate as necessary; many teacher preparation programs have declining enrollments. Under good management practice, when a decline in use does not seem to justify the expense of a separate curriculum materials center, consideration should be given to combining this unit with other media services, materials production service, or with the education library. Its use can thus actually be increased at the same time that economies are achieved through the sharing of personnel and facilities.

Conclusion

Although there may be wide diversity in organizational plans, administrative options, and personnel skills involved, a system to provide all curriculum support services is needed for teacher education programs. The curriculum materials center may contain all of the necessary services, but it is more likely to be the referral unit for coordinating all such services and the location of the curriculum materials collection.

NOTES

[1] National Council for the Accreditation of Teacher Education, Standards for Accreditation of Teacher Education (Washington, D.C.: National Association for the Accreditation of Teacher Education, 1979), p. 10.

[2] Ibid., p. 24.

[3] Royce P. Flandro, "Curriculum Laboratories in Colleges of Teacher Education" (Doctoral Dissertation, Indiana University, 1957), p. 72.

[4] Henry C. Meckel, interview, June 11, 1957, quoted in John Gideon Church, "The Development of Criteria for Evaluating Curriculum Laboratories in Teacher Education Institutions" (Doctoral Dissertation, University of Utah, 1957), p. 83.

[5]National Council for the Accreditation of Teacher Education, Standards for Accreditation, p. 10.

[6]Flandro, "Curriculum Laboratories, " p. 66.

[7]John Gideon Church, "The Development of Criteria for Evaluating Curriculum Laboratories in Teacher Education Institutions" (Doctoral Dissertation, University of Utah, 1957), pp. 13, 115.

[8]Murray G. Phillips, "Instructional Materials Centers: the Rationale, " in Instructional Materials Centers: Selected Readings, eds. Neville P. Pearson and Lucius Butler (Minneapolis: Burgess Publishing Company, 1969), p. 21.

[9]Flandro, "Curriculum Laboratories, " p. 81.

[10]Cora Paul Bomar, M. Ann Heidbreder and Carol A. Nemeyer, Guide to the Development of Educational Media Selection Centers (Chicago: American Library Association, 1976), pp. 57-58.

[11]Flandro, "Curriculum Laboratories, " p. 57.

[12]John Gideon Church, "Creating a Curriculum Laboratory, " California Education 1 (February, 1965): 22.

[13]Louise Stull and Edward G. Holley, "Some Materials Centers in the Midwest, " Journal of Teacher Education 11 (December, 1960): 570.

CHAPTER 3

THE CURRICULUM LABORATORY

Definition of the Laboratory Role of the Curriculum
Materials Center

One of the criticisms made of curriculum materials
centers administered by the academic library is that those
centers function as libraries and not as curriculum laboratories. A study of 303 instructional materials centers found
that a significant number of them did not appear to be ful-
filling their complete function:

> The responses of the 24 per cent on this question
> reveal a misconception of the function and purpose
> of this facility. Curriculum development personnel
> are not needed if the curriculum laboratory is
> treated as a library or branch library. There will
> be a waste of time and personnel and finance if
> this facility should operate or function as a library.
> There would be duplication of holdings, services,
> and other functions which would not enhance the to-
> tal college or university program. The curriculum
> laboratory will defeat its purpose should it fall short
> of its aims and objectives.[1]

Before criticizing curriculum materials centers for
failing in part of their duties, it is important to understand
just what the laboratory function is in today's curriculum materials center. Traditionally the activities of curriculum laboratories were those listed in a U.S. Office of Education Bulletin published in 1938. Of the activities listed, several seem
to be directly related to curriculum development rather than
to library services:

> 2.   Producing curriculum materials
> 3.   Advising and directing curriculum work

. . . .

6. Offering courses in the curriculum
7. Sponsoring curriculum conferences[2]

The study by Ellis listed some of the non-library functions that should be included in the services of the curriculum materials center. These include such functions as providing materials production services, collecting information on curriculum development, producing curriculum publications for the local and state education community, providing for research in the field of curricular materials, acting as a consultant in curriculum materials, and keeping close contact with the state education department on common concerns.[3]

Nevil in 1975 came to a conclusion that seems to have been close to the actual situation in the modern curriculum center, even though it is still not entirely accepted in theory: "The opinion was generally held that the curriculum laboratory should not take an active part in curriculum revision. The opinion was about evenly divided between those who thought that the curriculum laboratory should give aid to others for making curriculum revisions ... [or] made materials available for others to make their own curricular revisions."[4] Flandro had reached a similar conclusion as long ago as 1957: "Most curriculum laboratories in colleges of teacher education emphasize and may continue to emphasize the evaluation, procurement, cataloging, and housing of curriculum materials as well as maintain facilities to enable other educators to conduct their own curriculum study and revision."[5]

A realistic working definition of the curriculum center's role as a curriculum laboratory may be as the provider of those functions not usually provided as traditional library services and which play an active and direct part in assisting teachers and student teachers to develop the curriculum for classroom teaching.

As part of this laboratory role, the curriculum materials center continues its emphasis on teaching materials but also:

1. Works closely with the faculty in teacher training departments to make students familiar with the specialized materials which relate to teaching

2. Provides advice, instruction, facilities and raw
    material for graphic and audiovisual production
3. Understands current education concerns and
    assists students in the use of materials relating
    to these matters.

Support for the Professional Education Faculty

The professional personnel should be knowledgeable
and interested in the developments taking place in the field
of professional education. Regular reading in professional
journals and attendance at conferences, lectures, workshops,
or formal coursework are desirable. If the professional
staff members of the curriculum center are also involved in
selecting professional education materials, they will have an
advantage in keeping up with the field. The most direct
means of learning what will concern the education students
is through close liaison with the teaching faculty.

As in most academic library service, a good relationship with the teaching faculty makes it possible to play a key
role in motivating students to use the collection, and to gain
a better knowledge and understanding of the teaching documents which they are learning to prepare in their class work.
In order to develop a close relationship with the teaching
faculty, several techniques can be employed by the curriculum materials center personnel:

1. Know the instructional program thoroughly by
    reading the college catalog and attempting to
    collect detailed information about the curriculum
2. Ask teachers for copies of course outlines and
    reading lists and collect other handouts from
    the college dean or department chairperson.
    Use these to keep up with current education
    concerns and to identify where in the course
    curriculum materials might be used
3. Attend as many education faculty meetings as
    permitted
4. Ask for permission to visit classes where ap-
    propriate. If the course outline indicates some
    possible use of the center, seek an invitation
    to provide a tour or lecture on the center and
    its services
5. Let education faculty know that the director of
    the center is available as a consultant for cur-

riculum committees or for school curriculum
development activities such as state textbook
evaluation groups
6. Ask for faculty advice on purchases of items
for the collection and report back when the
items are ready for use
7. Prepare and send to faculty lists of the bibliographies in the center's reference collection
that are particularly appropriate for students in
an area of specialization
8. Cultivate personal relationships through coffee
breaks, faculty club activities, and other informal university activities. Use these occasions
to learn about current content of the academic
courses and new developments in the field.

Specialized Curriculum Materials

The basic collection of curriculum materials is primarily in printed form. These materials include curriculum
guides (including courses of study, research on teaching
units, and lesson plans); textbooks; periodicals; workbooks;
bibliographies and selection tools for curriculum materials,
and sources for purchase, rental, or borrowing; pamphlets;
manuals and how-to-do-it guides; publishers' catalogs;
children's encyclopedias and other reference materials suitable for school library media centers; and guides to free and
inexpensive materials. Among the ephemeral and unpublished
categories of materials which the curriculum materials center
might collect are:

Annual reports of school districts
Mimeographed bibliographies
Community surveys
Courses of study
Curriculum guides
Teaching units
Lesson Plans
Evaluations of schools and colleges (NCATE reports
and reports of regional accrediting agencies)
Pictures and photographs
Mounted graphs, photographs and pictures
Posters and charts
Plans for field trips and tourist guides
School report forms (samples of well-designed
forms)

Tests (standardized and from individual schools and
teachers)
Tapes (locally produced).

Librarians who are involved in one way or another
with the administration of the curriculum materials collection
should be familiar with certain categories of materials, the
definitions of which are well known to people in the field of
education, but which are not always clearly understood by
those outside the field. The following types of materials, of
great importance in the curriculum collection and briefly described here, are more completely defined in Good's Dictionary of Education:[6]

1. Course of study. A course of study is a document which a school, school district or state
education department prepares as a statement
to teachers on what is expected to be included
in the scope, content, and objectives for the
teaching of a subject. It may be for one grade
level, for several grades, or for the complete
kindergarten through twelfth grade program.
It may include curriculum guides, suggested
units, bibliographies of teaching aids, and
tests.
2. Curriculum guide. A curriculum guide is a
plan for presenting all or part of a course,
often prepared by a teacher and including ideas
on methods, objectives, materials to be used,
and a means for evaluation.
3. Teachers' handbook. Teachers are given a
handbook by the school or school district which
explains rules and regulations of the school,
required meetings, reports, school records,
and other practical information they will need
to conform to the particular policies and practices of the school.
4. Resource unit. A resource unit is a collection
of materials on a particular subject area from
which a teacher may select items for preparing
a teaching unit. It may contain content materials, methods, ideas for projects, field trips,
tests, lists of objectives, and bibliographies of
related materials.
5. Teaching unit. A teaching unit, more specific
than a resource unit, is a collection of the
ideas, plans, materials, evaluations, tests, and

other items needed for the actual teaching of the content of a portion of the subject matter.

6. Unit. A unit is a portion of the content of a course which represents a breakdown of the learning experiences, presentation of concepts, and material covered into manageable elements. The unit involves an integrated, often interdisciplinary, approach to the material to be presented and uses specific performance objectives, a plan for reaching the objectives, methods of presentation, and a means of evaluating the success of the unit.

7. Textbook. A textbook is a book designed to contain the subject content for a full course of study. A teacher's edition of a textbook contains the same content as the student's plus ideas, questions and answers, and suggestions for using the material effectively.

8. Teacher's manual. A teacher's manual is a guide for the teacher, often accompanying a textbook, and giving practical how-to-do-it suggestions for teaching a specific subject.

9. Workbook. A workbook is a group of practice exercises for the student to use in developing skills, and provides repetition, drill, and testing on material presented elsewhere. It may accompany a textbook, audiovisual or other teaching aid.

In popular usage, courses of study and curriculum guides are sometimes combined under the single rubric, curriculum guide.

A curriculum materials center has a library function of lending or otherwise distributing curriculum materials. As a laboratory, it also analyzes, evaluates, edits, and reviews curriculum materials, teaches students in education to do these tasks, and aids its patrons in performing them. The center carries out these operations by making itself the focus for information on curriculum, learning the local and state resources and needs, and acquiring local, national, and international resources.

In many cases the users of the center contribute to the information resources. They complete evaluation forms which build an evaluation file and help others in the examination of textbooks and other materials. They contribute copies

of unit plans and courses of study. They place on exhibit
well-designed productions of learning centers, bulletin board
designs, and other graphic material. They provide copies
of well-produced multi-media programs.

Curriculum Guides

In some school systems, it is necessary from time to
time that teachers provide a written curriculum document
which is a plan of what they are going to teach and how they
plan to teach it. A librarian trying to serve teachers in this
activity needs to understand the process. By knowing what
the teacher is attempting to do, the librarian will be better
able to help in the selection of material or in a plan for production.

In essence the teacher is creating an overall plan
which will have a specific goal of content knowledge. The
plan will set behavioral objectives, select activities to help
the students meet them, select the resources to support the
activities, and determine ways to evaluate the process on a
continuing basis and overall. Each step will also need to be
defined as to content, behavioral objectives, methodology,
resources, and evaluation. In education, behavioral objectives
are usually stated in terms of a student performing an activity under certain conditions in a certain time period, the desired goal being a successful grasp of the concept taught.
A rather simple example, indicating the behavioral objective
of a spelling drill, might be:

Student	Conditions	Activity	Time
A second grader	From a list of 5 possible choices	Will choose the correct spelling of the word	After 5 minutes of drill

The Instructional Objectives Exchange (IOX) publishes collections of behavioral objectives and statements to match almost
any curriculum. Its catalog is available from Box 24095,
Los Angeles, California 90024.

Very often the methodology and materials employed in
building a curriculum document are complicated by the teacher's knowledge of his or her own strengths and limitations,
which are, of course, the most important resource involved
in the process. Teachers may tend to use only those teach-

ing techniques which reflect their own best skills. Exposure to a variety of methods and media help to counteract this. Another complication is the need to determine that the content and ideas follow a logical sequence and, if possible, relate to more than one discipline. Here the curriculum center can help by providing access to the sample plans of other researchers, which can help in the development of the teacher's own curriculum document.

The activities which the teacher chooses should include a broad spectrum of learning modes so that children who fail to learn from one mode can grasp the ideas presented through another. This is especially important in cases where students have physical handicaps that might prevent them from getting the most from any one mode. For a student with visual handicaps listening exercises are a necessity. The activities need to follow a sequence that presents ideas and experiences which build upon each other and lead toward both the minor objectives and the overall goal.

There are often limitations which must be accepted and the reference librarian helping a student teacher will need to know about these before suggesting materials. There may be time or scheduling restrictions, for example, or limits on space or equipment. Clearly it is not sensible to suggest a rental film for a teacher whose needs are immediate, or the production of a complex learning center for use in the next week, or active games in a crowded classroom. Some restrictions occur because of content relationships with other disciplines or to other grade levels. Extensive intentional duplication of what is taught by another teacher to a child at another time has to be avoided. Budget restrictions may be a limitation, perhaps precluding the use of supplies for producing certain materials.

The selection of materials appropriate to the curriculum may be very important because it can often assist the teacher in developing more or better ideas or activities. When curriculum materials in all formats are shelved together, a variety of approaches is suggested and brought to the student teacher's attention.

The evaluation part of the plan should provide some immediate feedback to the student--the winning of a game or completion of a learning center program--and also have some objective measures for the overall success of the plan. The behavioral objectives should be met, at least to some extent, by all of the children involved.

Very often the document which the teacher prepares becomes a curriculum guide and is useful to other teachers. If possible the librarian should urge teachers to deposit such guides in the curriculum center's files. It is also important to remind teachers that these guides, produced either by an individual or by groups of teachers, be deposited in the ERIC data base. For maximum access via catalogs and automated indexing, a descriptive title and a well-prepared abstract are important. The ERIC data base has proven to be an excellent and inexpensive source for locating curriculum guides, and it serves the purpose of distributing the work of individuals or small groups to a wider audience. Both guides for long-range courses and those for single issues at one grade level are valid and useful--the long-range plan providing the overall program and the work unit being especially useful for an integrated approach to current issues. Users of curriculum guide collections often ask for such topics as bilingual education, values education, developmental education, or core curriculum.

Librarians in charge of the curriculum collection need to know what is expected of curriculum guides. These guides serve several functions in helping teachers decide what to teach and how to teach it. For example, a curriculum guide on the energy shortage might provide a coordinated basis for integrating instruction in science and social science around a central theme. Such a guide could form the basis for the development of resource or teaching units. Thus it could be useful to the teacher who would use it for his or her own individual interpretation.

Some of the more general courses of study and curriculum guides are prepared by curriculum committees on a system or statewide basis. Some states provide a fairly well-integrated set for use statewide; these are based on a rigid syllabus of requirements for each subject at each grade level. All states have at least some activity in this area, in order to provide standards for schools and to articulate the content of the curriculum from one grade level to another. The production of curriculum guides is not confined to departments of education and instruction. Other state agencies develop curriculum guides to foster instruction in their particular subject interests, such as public health, safety, or environmental concerns. An extensive state or school system program of preparing curriculum guides can set standards for content and levels of instruction while at the same time allowing for the individual teacher's interpretation. Some of the general course-of-study guides organize a whole subject into a plan for total instruction from kindergarten through the twelfth grade. Others are designed for a group such as elementary grades or for a single grade level.

Some curriculum materials centers shelve courses of study and curriculum guides separately. Often, however, they are grouped together, and the term "curriculum guide" is used to indicate both types. The two types of publication are hard to separate, since courses of study may include elements which are essentially curriculum guides for specific areas of instruction.

The goals of the general type of guide are usually broad, but the guide will define the specific organization for reaching those goals. Such guides may include behavioral objectives, suggested units for one or more grades, or lists of curriculum materials, and suggest various methods for teaching the content. Plans for experiments, guided reading lists, audiovisual presentations, and field trips may be included as well as ideas for using writing exercises, dramatizations, or art work. These guides should contain:

1. Their purpose for existing
2. Their scope (subject and level)
3. Specific objectives (knowledge, practice, skills, research)
4. Plans and suggestions for resource units (organized for meeting the objectives).

Some curriculum guides, even for such interdisciplinary topics as solar energy or freedom of the press, are very specific; they should, nevertheless, be used only as guides and examples for teachers preparing their own plans. The hierarchy for curriculum development proceeds from the broad to the specific, and teachers' preparations for class go from a course of study to a curriculum guide, to a research and/or teaching unit, to lesson plans, and ultimately to single concepts. Education students have learned to prepare these documents in their course work. It is, however, of benefit to supplement the theory of the classroom with good examples, before the students have to begin the actual construction of plans for themselves. It is, therefore, important that the center keep good examples of each of the above types of material on file so that students can examine them in detail, compare them to the theoretical requirements, and understand the various components before preparing their own examples. When the curriculum center works closely with the faculty who teach methods and curriculum courses, this can be especially valuable. A system for depositing copies of the outstanding work of students can also be set up with the cooperation of interested faculty.

At all times the individual creativity of the teacher should be stressed, echoing "the view that the proper function of the instructional bulletin is to serve as an aid to be used voluntarily by the teacher, not as a prescribed course of study to be followed rigidly. "[7]

Given the nature of the curriculum development process, the role of the curriculum materials center as a curriculum laboratory is very important. That role is not, however, without problems. One problem is the physical form of many curriculum guides; they are often in microfiche from published sets or from ERIC. Or they may be mimeographed and poorly edited or produced. Even where the technical production of the publication is excellent, all too often a spiral binding is used. This has the advantage of being inexpensive and makes it easy for teachers to photocopy selected parts for research use or classroom purposes, but a wire or plastic back does create a storage problem. Spiral backs are hard to organize on shelves, will not stand alone, and have a tendency to hook together in pamphlet files. In vertical files, the complications of broken plastic and wire backs tangled together make this physical form very frustrating both to staff and to users of the collection. At least one center has bound its collection, using color coding for the source of the publication; all state curriculum guides, for example, are one color. The difficulties of handling and protecting this physical format may be one reason why microfiche collections are popular even though they do not usually provide the local and very current approach most desired by curriculum guide users.

Some research has been done on what materials are most used in curriculum materials centers. Donald MacVean found the most widely used materials were courses of study, textbooks, teachers' manuals and units of work, in that order. [8] St. Cyr found that the most popular items were first the textbooks, then units of work, courses of study and pamphlets. [9]

The Production of Curriculum Materials

Flandro's study found that there was "a close relationship between the production of curriculum materials and
the construction of curriculum itself."[10] Student teachers
soon find out that the best materials to meet the specific
teaching problems they encounter are those which they design
and produce to meet their own immediate and particular
needs. Also, because of time restrictions, they may have
to use materials that are locally produced. An ideal situation is the one in which the student teacher can describe
what is needed and have an expert production person do the
actual creation. Most instructional media production programs on the campus, however, offer this kind of complete
service only to the university or college faculty, or on a very
low priority to student teachers. The student is then thrown
back onto the resources of the curriculum center. Student
teachers have learned the skills of materials production as
part of their course work and should know how to create such
things as posters, simple learning centers, transparencies
and other graphic forms, as well as the more complex details
of audiovisual production. The personnel in the curriculum
materials library should not be just keepers of a storehouse
of teaching aids but should also be actively involved in assisting students in finding the means for preparing the materials
they need to use in practice teaching.

Educational media may take a variety of different
forms, many of which can be produced in the production center of the curriculum materials library. The production facilities may not actually be located physically in the immediate area of the curriculum collection. Graphics production
or electronic media production are often separate units in the
system and may not even be administratively a part of the library. Just as frequently either or both production facilities
are immediately adjacent to, or are a part of, the materials
collection facility. This is for the good reason that the production department needs many of the resources in the collection: instruction books and manuals on producing education
materials, idea books or things to create, pictures, maps,
and graphs needed for reproduction in multi-media programs,
and examples of materials similar to those being produced.

It is useful to identify and classify the various types
of media that might be produced. Visual media include the
still forms such as print, pictures, photographs, graphics
and slides, as well as the moving forms such as film, tele-

vision pictures and computer screens. Audio forms include
tapes, discs, and cassettes as well as remote transmission
forms such as radio, telephone, or the sound track of video
production. These forms also come in various audiovisual
combinations, such as sound filmstrips, books with accompanying cassettes, sound film or video. Kits may include
several of these forms together. Two other types of media
widely used in curriculum collections are games, which teach
by a form of interaction, and realia, which are the basis for
observational learning. Educational realia may take many
forms. Among them are print and graphics in three-dimensional form, such as a globe or alphabet blocks. Other
realia include such items as musical instruments, toys, scale
models, mineral samples, counting devices, and even goldfish
or rabbits.

Retrievable media form another grouping, including,
for example, dial access to listening center tapes or to a
telecommunications system. Terminals serving as access to
computer systems, or word-processing typewriter terminals
linked to a central processor and file, also fall in this category. The growth of the network concept makes this category a growing source of information, and terminals to
search the library's circulation system or the ERIC data base
are reasonable additions to a curriculum materials center in
an academic institution.

Pictures and graphics have played a large part in
classroom teaching for many years. Even the most formal
classroom, long before this century, had illustrations from
the classics, maps mounted on the wall, and a chalkboard.
In developing curriculum, the teacher or pre-teacher is often
interested in the manipulation of graphic forms in such a way
that they can become part of a teaching unit. Curriculum collections contain a wide variety of graphic materials: maps,
charts, art prints, study prints, flash cards, posters, photographs, and reproductions of documents. These are widely
used because of their ease of handling, their versatility, and
their contribution to producing original combinations in the
creation of multi-media productions or learning centers for
individual instruction. Sets of visuals in card or poster form
may demonstrate mathematical sets, word-picture recognition,
or the physical environment of natural and manufactured items.
The use of pictures of farm life to be studied by city children
is an example of the latter. Commercially produced materials combined with locally designed graphics are commonly
used in assembling bulletin boards or display cases as teach-

ing devices. Student-produced materials are especially effective and teachers need to know how to use projectors to trace on the chalkboard enlargements of small visuals that children produce. This practice could have copyright ramifications, however, if published materials are used in this way. Metal chalkboards that allow the use of magnets for displaying visuals, easels, hanging displays, mobiles, and models are among other items that challenge the student teacher to produce, or to help children in classes to produce good visuals.

Pictures and graphics can also be projected by using opaque projectors or by transferring the material to transparency or slide form and using an overhead or slide projector. The opaque projection process, whatever its equipment limitations and requirements for total darkness, is still the only way to project for group viewing a full-color image of a picture or book page when closed circuit television is not available.

Slides and filmstrips are a good way to present sequential pictures or graphics. Filmstrips are less expensive and many commercially produced filmstrips are available. However, filmstrips are less adaptable and do not have the flexibility of slides, so students often prefer to make their own productions in slide form. Both forms are easily stored--the filmstrips in cylindrical cans or plastic containers, and the slides in boxes or projection trays or cassettes. While slides in the $3\frac{1}{4}$" x 4" size have a brighter image on the screen, the 2" x 2" size, popular with amateur photographers, is most commonly used. These visual media are often combined with sound recordings and sound filmstrips, or slide-tape programs are projected either remotely or on a built-in rear-vision screen. Equipment designed for the combined function is available, or separate pieces can be synchronized to work together. Sound recordings are produced on reel-to-reel tape, cassettes, 8-track cassettes, or discs. These can be locally recorded, but in many cases local recordings are the result of converting small segments from various forms of commercially produced music. Such recording for classroom use, if temporary and erased after use, is commonly interpreted as fair use under the copyright law. A greater variety of commercially produced material is still available on discs, but tapes are more common in locally produced sound recording, because they are easier to duplicate and repair, and because they wear better.

Programmed instruction is another medium which may be offered in the curriculum collection and which students may learn to produce. Programmed instruction offers small bits of information in a structured format, with immediate evaluation and feedback to the student. It usually offers the student the choice of several presentations of the concepts and a selection of answers to questions that are posed for evaluation. If the concept is not understood, it is presented in another example or in a different format. The best form of programmed instruction is computer-assisted instruction (CAI), because of the infinite variability of the computer. While terminals should be provided in a curriculum center to introduce education students to this form of teaching, the role of the center is often to refer the students to another source where they can find out what programs are available locally in CAI and how to gain access to them. Curriculum materials centers usually provide programmed instruction in other forms on various types of teaching machines. Education students need to be aware that some teaching machine manufacturers will convert the programs they have written to the format needed for use on the manufacturers equipment. Programmed instruction may be in book form also, and it is useful for small segments of learning such as introducing a new concept or providing practice on small units of knowledge which build toward broader understanding.

Because of its high cost, 16mm film is largely ignored in most curriculum collections except for demonstrations on how to use the equipment. Some samples may be provided and used for this purpose. For previewing a rental film or one being considered for purchase, rear vision projectors are available for use by one person or a small group. This type of projector has a built-in screen. The high cost of 16mm film makes the development of a large collection economically impossible for most institutions, and student production facilities seldom offer it. Instead, the curriculum center provides catalogs and lists from institutions where 16mm film can be rented or purchased. The center does not usually provide a rental service itself except in cases where the center also handles the general library's audiovisual services. Students who are eligible to rent films are usually referred to the university-wide film rental service or to such a service in the school where their teaching practicum will be done.

Some of the uses of published materials in the production center raise copyright issues. The section on educational media in The New Copyright Law: Questions Teachers and Librarians Ask offers some basic guidance on this matter. Teachers and librarians need to keep abreast of court decisions as case law develops under the copyright law of 1976. Several of the answers given in The New Copyright Law are based on legislative intent, and stress that the "excerpt" can be copied but not the whole work, that excerpts to create an anthology would be a violation, and that use of copied materials should be confined to spontaneous classroom use. Guidelines for recording from instructional television programs have been defined by a group of agencies. [11] Copying from any commercial product for production of classroom materials should be done with caution, and a determination made as to whether or not the copying really does fall within the "fair use" definition for research and education. At the same time unnecessary restrictions should not be placed on the use of materials for education. In the academic library, good policies have usually been developed to handle copyright concerns, and this is an area where the curriculum center benefits from its association with the library organization.

Other sources of information on copyright rules for the copying of materials for educational use are:

> Johnston, Donald. Copyright Handbook. New York: Bowker, 1978.
> Miller, Jerome K. Applying the New Copyright Law: A Guide for Educators and Librarians. Chicago: American Library Association, 1979.
> Lawrence, John Shelton and Timberg, Bernard. Fair Use and Free Inquiry. Norwood, N.J.: Ablex Publishing Corporation, 1980.

The last title has some particularly good selections which discuss the copyright ramifications of duplicating visual and graphic materials as a part of the design of instructional materials.

The functions of the curriculum center become interrelated in the production area. The technological functions of taking pictures, developing film, or video-taping may require use of the picture file, information on copyright restrictions, and manuals for producing teaching aids. The collection should provide assistance for such needs.

All the pre-teachers and teachers using the curriculum center are not likely to become expert script writers, camera

operators, directors, or video technologists, but they will
all need to know enough about the technology to meet their
own teaching needs. The high school chemistry teacher
should know enough to prepare a video-tape of the preparation of the glassware set up for a chemistry laboratory class
so that the students can view it before the lab session and
save time in preparing their own equipment for experiments.

The education students will have learned that the approach to selecting the correct media forms should be based
on a rational pattern of analyzing the subject matter, developing the objectives, determining which media form or forms
best suit the situation, selecting or designing appropriate
media, and fitting them into an effective mode of instruction
in a unit plan or lesson plans. After the instruction has
taken place, the media used should be evaluated along with
other parts of the unit plan. Not all curriculum materials
centers will do all of the following instruction, but some help
on these items should be available to students, either directly
or by referral:

1. How to select the proper form of media for
   teaching a concept
2. The use of equipment
3. How to obtain media items
4. How to produce media materials
5. How to use media effectively
6. What other media resources are available on
   campus
7. How to rent audiovisual items
8. How to get free media items
9. How to preview for purchase
10. How to evaluate and select equipment.

A director of a curriculum collection who is both a
librarian and an education graduate should have had formal
course work in media production and the use of educational
technology in the classroom setting. It is probably still desirable that a number of college textbooks or manuals on the
use of multimedia be available in the collection. They can
be helpful in updating and refreshing the memories of the
professional staff, and in staff training; they will also, of
course, serve as a quick resource for the users of the production center. This collection might include such titles as
Doing the Media: A Portfolio of Activities, Ideas and Resources (Revised edition, Kit Laybourne and Pauline Ciancolo,
eds., New York: McGraw-Hill, 1978). The center's person-

nel must have a good knowledge of all related services on
the campus and also of the professional literature in the library's collection.   Users of the center need to realize how
much overlap in content there may be with materials in the
professional education collection, and they need to be re-
minded that some periodicals primarily devoted to professional articles may also contain curriculum ideas and projects.

The materials production laboratory should be able to
provide lettering devices, recording equipment (audio and
video), synthesizers, playback equipment, duplicators, typewriters, slide sequence illuminators, photography equipment,
video production equipment, portable lighting equipment,
mounting and laminating equipment, story boards or planning
boards, and all kinds of art and graphic supplies.

Planning boards and cards are often used to create a
script or to evaluate and plan the transition to units of an
audiovisual program.   Cards are placed on a planning board
where transparent plastic strips hold 30-40 cards.   Cards
can easily be added, shifted, or withdrawn, and space left
for brief statements or sample illustrations or sketches.
Both boards and cards are available from Numbatabs, P. O.
Box 44, Rochester, New York 14601, or a homemade board
can be built.   Directions for making a planning board appear
in Kodak Publication No. S-11, Audiovisual Planning Equipment, available from the Kodak Motion Picture and Audiovisual Markets Division, Rochester, New York 14650.

The Kodak publications are very useful in the curriculum center regardless of whether the service includes actual
multimedia production or is just teaching students or teachers to use materials for their work in an audiovisual production facility elsewhere on campus.   For example, the pamphlet mentioned above also includes directions for making a
slide sequence illuminator--a device for arranging, editing,
and inspecting slides against a lighted glass background.
Sources for purchase of slide-sequence illuminators are also
given.   Other useful titles in the Kodak series are Effective
Lecture Slides, Materials for Visual Presentations: Planning
and Preparation, and Legibility--Artwork to Screen.

Production Space

A frequent complaint from personnel in instructional

media production centers is lack of sufficient space. They
cite the need to give students room to work on and store
elaborate learning centers, each of which may require a
large table or involve building a structure using 3-ply construction board. The learning center may take diverse
forms, such as a playhouse or an airplane where the student
sits in the cockpit to read. Adequate work space is very important.

Learning centers in the classroom came about as a
result of the emphasis on the open school with individualized
curriculum and emphasis on relevant content and empirical
assignments. A learning center is an instructional aid which
is developed to provide an individual learning experience
which accomplishes a concept goal or develops a skill at the
ability level of the individual student. Learning centers supply direct experiences in a structured situation through reading, listening, observing, handling, and manipulating materials which facilitate learning. The best of these stimulate
creativity, provide variety, and personalize the program,
thus providing an alternative to the formal classroom curriculum.

The role of the teacher is to prepare the learning
center by defining the subject, skill and concepts to be
learned, introducing it to the student, and interacting with
the student on a one-to-one basis to monitor progress, moti-
vate effective use, and evaluate the results. Sometimes one
or more children are involved in creating a learning center
or in adding new elements to an existing program. Some
learning centers are meant to be used by a group but are
not under the immediate supervision of the teacher in a traditional classroom exercise.

The spatial element of the learning center in the
school situation is important since it provides a dedicated
space for one set of activities, creates a private work and
study space, or sets up an exhibit area, a tabletop work
space or a place for individualized media projection. Boxes,
platforms, and curtained-off areas break up the open space.
For this reason learning centers are particularly useful in
the open classroom concept of education where flexible grouping of students based on a variety of ability levels made
rooms unnecessary for many activities and the classroom
without walls a possibility for some teaching/learning purposes. While the return to basics has placed greater emphasis on general classroom drill in reading, composition, and

mathematics, the learning center continues to have an important role in providing additional skill exercises to those who need more practice, extra stimulation for students who learn more quickly than their group, and especially the variety of teaching modes needed for the mainstreaming of handicapped students into the classroom situation.

It is important that the curriculum materials center, regardless of its production activities, provide help to students who are being taught to prepare learning centers. Some good examples of manuals which provide a wide variety of ideas for learning centers on all subjects are:

> Change for Children: Ideas and Activities for
> Individualized Learning. Sandra Nina Kaplan;
> Jo Ann Butom Kaplan; Shiela Kunishima Madsen; and Bette K. Taylor. Santa Monica,
> California: Goodyear Publishing Company, Inc.,
> 1973.
> Clendening, Corinne P. and Ruth Ann Davies.
> Creating Programs for the Gifted: A Guide for
> Teachers, Librarians and Students. New York:
> Bowker, 1980.
> The Learning Center Book: an Integrated Approach.
> Tom Davidson; Phyllis Fountain; Rachell
> Grogan; Verl Short; and Judy Steely. Santa
> Monica, California: Goodyear Publishing Company, Inc., 1976.

The curriculum center which operates primarily as a library can also provide space for exhibiting good learning centers produced by the students. This can be interesting displays and effective examples for students seeking information to use in building a learning center.

Special Issues in the Curriculum Development Process

As active participants in the development of curriculum by students and teachers, the personnel of the curriculum center should be well aware of the special issues which complicate the curriculum development process. Issues frequently show up in the reference interview when student teachers are developing plans for their classroom instruction. Frequent questions involve issues such as mainstreaming and values education. The curriculum center personnel need to be aware that other issues will arise, and be prepared to respond promptly when information is sought on a new issue in education.

Mainstreaming

Mainstreaming of handicapped children into the regular classroom has been ordered by Public Law 94-142, The Education of All Handicapped Children Act. Mainstreaming as a term means that whenever it is appropriate and meaningful for an individual child, he or she will be placed in the regular school classroom. Under PL 94-142, professionals working with handicapped children must develop an Individualized Education Program (IEP) for each child in cooperation with the child's parents. The IEP must:

1. Appear in written format
2. Describe the child's present level of educational performance
3. State annual goals
4. State short-term instructional objectives
5. Describe specific educational services to be provided
6. Describe the extent of the child's ability to participate in regular educational programs
7. Determine the starting date of the child's program
8. Anticipate the duration of the services
9. Select appropriate objective criteria and evaluation procedures to determine whether instructional objectives are being achieved
10. Determine the schedule for evaluating progress, at least annually. [12]

While the preparation and monitoring of the IEP may fall upon a caseworker or special education teacher, the classroom teacher is involved in the plan and takes a major role in the program's implementation, very often providing individualized instruction units based on the handicap of the child.

The curriculum center should have a variety of materials, including teaching aids designed for many different types of handicaps, and fiction which helps other children understand and accept handicapped children. While a wide variety of commercial publications is becoming available for these purposes, the teacher may use learning centers to provide needed specialized individual training aids.

Stanley Swartz has suggested that teachers will have
to prepare themselves in several ways, one of which is in
the modifying of methods and materials.   He suggests that:

> Others will need the use of different materials,
> devices, or sensory modalities to circumvent their
> handicaps.   An evaluation will need to be made of
> the presently available materials and how they
> might be adapted for use with handicapped children.
> New materials specifically designed for the handi-
> capped child will need to be identified.   More at-
> tention to individualized learning styles and prob-
> lems will be necessary.   An overall increase in
> flexibility, in both types and use of instructional
> materials, holds great promise of success. [13]

This need is an obvious challenge which the academic
library curriculum center should be taking a leadership role
in meeting.   The Instructional Materials Center Network for
Handicapped Children and Youth has fourteen regional centers
which are sources of information.   Some specialize in one
type of handicap; for example, there is one in Kentucky which
specializes in the visually handicapped and one in Florida
which specializes in the mentally retarded, emotionally disturbed, and speech impaired.   Most, however, cover all
types of physical, mental, and emotional handicaps.   The academic curriculum center should have, besides its samples of
special materials, bibliographies of more such material in its
reference collection, and printed brochures and information
from the many associations concerned with education of handicapped children.   Some of these agencies are:

Alexander Graham Bell Association for the Deaf,
    3417 Volta Place, Washington, D. C. 20017
American Association for Children with Learning
    Disabilities, 4156 Library Road, Pittsburgh,
    Pennsylvania 15234
American Association on Mental Deficiency, 5101
    Wisconsin Avenue N. W. , Washington, D. C.
    20016
American Foundation for the Blind, 15 W. Sixteenth
    Street, New York, New York 10011
Association for Education of the Visually Handi-
    capped, 919 Walnut Street, Philadelphia, Penn-
    sylvania 19107
Closer Look, National Information Center of the
    Handicapped, P. O. Box 1492, Washington,
    D. C. 20013

Convention of American Instructors of the Deaf,
5034 Wisconsin Avenue N. W. , Washington,
D. C. 20016

Council for Exceptional Children, 1920 Association
Drive, Reston, Virginia 22091

Epilepsy Foundation of America, 1828 L Street,
N. W. , Suite 406, Washington, D. C. 20026

Instructional Materials Reference Center, American
Printing House for the Blind, 1839 Frankfort
Avenue, Louisville, Kentucky 40208

International Reading Association, 800 Parkdale Rd. ,
Newark, Delaware 19711

Literacy Volunteers of America, Inc. , 6th Floor,
Midtown Plaza, 700 E. Water Street, Syracuse,
New York 13201

Muscular Dystrophy Association, 810 Seventh Avenue, New York, New York 10019

National Association for Retarded Citizens, 2709
Avenue E East, Arlington, Texas 79011

National Association for the Visually Handicapped,
3201 Balboa Street, San Francisco, California
94121

National Information Center for Special Education
Materials, University of Southern California,
University Park, Los Angeles, California 90007

National Jewish Hospital/National Asthma Center,
Department of Communications, 3800 E. Colfax
Avenue, Denver, Colorado 80206

Orton Society, 8415 Vellona Lane, Suite 113, Tow-
son, Maryland 21204

Schools Department, American Speech and Hearing
Association, 9030 Old Georgetown Road,
Washington, D. C. 20014

United Cerebral Palsy Association, Program Services, Dept. 66, East 34th Street, New York,
New York 10016

Associations such as these can often provide lists of
materials for use both by the handicapped child and by other
students who need to understand and relate naturally to their
disabled classmates. A book by James G. Meade, The
Rights of Parents and the Responsibilities of Schools (Cam-
bridge, Mass.: Educators Publishing Service, 1978), is
helpful for general information on mainstreaming, and Education Unlimited, a journal devoted to mainstreaming, is available from Educational Resources Center, 1834 Meetinghouse
Road, Boothwyn, Pennsylvania 19061.

Sometimes the high interest, low vocabulary books are helpful in teaching children with handicaps, because their school progress may have been slowed by their handicaps. Special materials for the deaf include films and video tapes with captions. A teacher may wish to preview amplified recordings with a child who has a hearing handicap, so it is helpful if the curriculum materials center has at least one sound-proof room or carrel where this type of material can be played without other sound interference. The student teacher will want to have access to darkrooms, cameras and enlargers, typewriters with oversize type and printing and lettering equipment for use with children who can only use large print. One of the most effective aids in teaching students with a hearing handicap is CAI, and the curriculum materials specialists should be prepared to introduce this teaching mode to pre- and in-service teachers or refer them to other agencies which can do this. Because CAI is entirely visual and offers a printed dialog between the student and the program in the computer, it is ideal for giving instruction and practice which students with good hearing get in conversation.

Professional education students should be aware of the Visualtek Machine and the Edu Trainer Handicap Learning Center, both of which use closed circuit television to enlarge printed material onto a video screen and thus make small print materials usable by those who only read large print. The Kurzweil machine is another piece of equipment that future teachers should know about. It is a small desk-top computer which translates printed or typed writing into natural language, which it reads aloud to the child who has no vision. Brochures describing such mechanical aids to the handicapped should be a part of the vertical file collection.

Values Education

The wide variety of options in life styles in an open democratic society has led in recent years to the issue of values education as a part of the public school curriculum. Values education involves the teaching of individual emotions and personal relationships as they affect decision-making on moral, ethical, religious, and patriotic issues. Values education varies widely, from non-prejudicial exploration of beliefs to the teaching of certain values as the "right" beliefs and behavior in American society. There are wide disagreements about many of the values but in theory, at least, a belief in justice, equality of opportunity, human dignity, and freedom of choice are essential in a democratic state. Some of the elements involved in values education have to do with discussion and attention to moral questions as they arise, examining alternative values, building the child's self-esteem and awareness of his or her role in society, and encouraging the child to take responsibility and make decisions on behavior consistent with his or her own values.

Some curriculum materials are designed especially to bring moral and ethical issues to the child's attention, but often the issue as it relates to materials selection concerns the expression of a value system in materials such as textbooks. As a result, this issue often becomes an element in textbook censorship attempts.

Conclusion

Clearly, the curriculum materials center in the academic library still plays a role in the traditional laboratory function. Its collection and reference services provide the resources and advice that student teachers need as they go through the process of developing curriculum and creating the documents which represent this activity. The closely related activity of materials production is also supported by the center, either through the maintenance of an actual production center or by taking an active role in leading education students to instructional manuals, commercial sources for supplies, or appropriate production facilities available on campus or in the community. In directing the curriculum center's services as a curriculum laboratory, the professional staff must have expertise and awareness of concerns in the field of education. The most important contribution is still, however, the provision of an appropriate collection of materials needed for curriculum development.

NOTES

[1] Eleanor V. Ellis, The Role of the Curriculum Laboratory in the Preparation of Quality Teachers (ED 31457) (Tallahassee: Florida A&M Foundation, Inc., 1969), p. 57.

[2] Bernice E. Leary, Curriculum Laboratories and Divisions (Their Organization and Function in State Departments

of Education, City School Systems, and Institutions of Higher Education), Bulletin No. 7 (Washington, D.C.: U.S. Department of the Interior, Office of Education, 1938), pp. 16-17.

[3] Ellis, The Role of the Curriculum Laboratory, pp. 63-64.

[4] Leota Nevil, "A Survey of Curriculum Laboratories in Selected Colleges in Pennsylvania" (ED 112909) (Master's Thesis, Wilkes College, 1975), p. 68.

[5] Royce P. Flandro, "Curriculum Laboratories in Colleges of Teacher Education" (Doctoral Dissertation, Indiana University, 1957), p. 187.

[6] Dictionary of Education, ed. Carter V. Good, 3rd ed. (New York: McGraw-Hill Book Company, 1973).

[7] Henry Harap and E. Merritt, "Trends in the Production of Curriculum Guides," Educational Leadership 13 (October, 1955): 35.

[8] Donald MacVean, "Report of an Evaluation of Curriculum Laboratory Services in a Teachers College," Journal of Educational Research 53 (May, 1960): 342.

[9] Carol Ruth St. Cyr, "Present and Potential Uses of the University of Michigan Curriculum Materials Center" (Doctoral Dissertation, University of Michigan, 1955), p. 55.

[10] Flandro, "Curriculum Laboratories," p. 56.

[11] The New Copyright Law: Questions Teachers and Librarians Ask (Chicago: American Library Association, and Washington, D.C.: Association for Educational Communications and Technology, 1977), pp. 70-71.

[12] Stanley L. Swartz, "Mainstreaming News: The IEP Question," Curriculum Review 18 (August/September, 1979): 177-178.

[13] Stanley L. Swartz, "Zero Reject--The Public Law Regarding Handicapped Children," Curriculum Review 17 (October, 1978): 251-253.

CHAPTER 4

THE CURRICULUM MATERIALS CENTER AS A FACILITY

Standards

In 1975, the American Association of School Librarians and the Association for Educational Communication and Technology updated the previous standards for school library media center programs in their joint publication, Media Programs: District and School.[1] In this latest revision of the standards, the district media center was included as a reflection of the rapid development of cooperative collections to support the teaching functions with equipment and materials which schools might not be able to afford for individual purchase. Because of the similarity in functions between the district media center and curriculum collections located in academic libraries, these association guidelines are useful in the planning of facilities for the academic curriculum materials center. A study of district centers indicated that they range in size from 2000 to 8000 square feet.[2] The general guidelines in the AASL/AECT standards statement indicate that centers should be in the upper range of this size, or 4000 to 8000 square feet.[3] Johnson found the average size of academic curriculum materials centers which he visited during his study was 3960 square feet, but they ranged widely, from 2000 to 19,000 square feet.[4] The media programs standards give many quantitative values for functions in the school media center which are also applicable to the district center and to the academic curriculum materials center.

Another set of descriptive guidelines which can be usefully consulted appears in Guide to the Development of Educational Media Selection Centers.[5] The educational materials evaluation centers, where they have been implemented, provide to public schools some of the services which academic curriculum centers supply to their primary clientele and in

66

many locations influence the status of the academic centers
in teacher training institutions.

Since managers of curriculum centers often complain
more about inadequate facilities than about shortages of materials and personnel, standards indicating what is to be expected are important, even though there may be wide differences in functions which would cause substantial variations
in the needs of different curriculum centers. As long ago
as 1946, Francis Drag described what a curriculum laboratory required in the form of space and facilities. In a study
of 145 centers, Drag's conclusions were that "the laboratory
be located so as to utilize to the maximum the advantages of
the library as well as to permit all professional education
staff members ready access to the quarters and facilities of
the laboratory"; and that "sufficient space be provided not
only to store all types of materials, the resource and enrichment as well as the audio-visual, but also to provide for
the practice of curriculum discussion groups, curriculum
study of research efforts, and curriculum production activities."[6]

Location of the Center

When the curriculum materials center is administratively a part of the academic library, the decision whether
to locate the collection physically within the general or education library or in the professional education classroom
area requires a careful look at the advantages of both locations. St. Cyr reported that her research "showed a defi-
nite trend for desiring the curriculum materials and professional books to be more accessible to one another."[7] She
recommended the location for the University of Michigan
center: "The general consensus seems to be that the best
location for the Center is in the School of Education Building
in a room adjoining the School of Education Library."[8] Certainly the location of curriculum materials as part of the
professional education library works effectively in such
places as Washington State University and Sacramento State
University.

The factors leading to a decision on physical location
of the curriculum collection are similar to those influencing
a decision on administrative control. Location within the
college or school for teacher training is supported by good
reasons:

1. Convenience for the primary clientele
2. More faculty awareness and interest
3. Closer relationship to the professional education administration
4. More often including or near to the materials production center.

Depending upon the circumstances, there may be reasons why a library building or facility offers greater advantages as the physical location of the collection:

1. Proximity to professional education books and periodicals
2. Overlap with other audiovisual materials, some of which are suitable for secondary teaching
3. Proximity to library administrators, the source of the budget
4. Location of qualified substitute personnel nearby
5. Better security measures
6. Longer hours of service.

Some combinations of the above may form the basis for the location decision, or the following local conditions may result in one location being favored over the other:

1. The amount of good parking facilities nearby
2. The size of space available and possibilities for expansion
3. The suitability of space for electronic equipment
4. The traffic pattern to and from supporting agencies such as audiovisual services, video production area, or the testing center.

The location of the curriculum materials center might be communicated to an architect on the basis of its relationship to other supporting or supported services by creating a priority chart (see Fig. 1, p. 69).

Whatever political reasons there may be for locating the curriculum collection in space designed for library purposes, it can be located in a classroom adjacent to education classes if proper precautions are taken. In remodeled space, one of the most important considerations is provision for growth. The rate of growth of the collection will not usually be as rapid as normal library growth. If the collection is

```
LOCATION PRIORITY

(A = highest priority)

Supervision and Administration

  Near the college or department of education    A  B  C
  Near the library system                        A  B  C
  Near the library science program               A  B  C

High Traffic

  Related classes

    Methods or curriculum                        A  B  C
    Materials Production                         A  B  C
    Equipment instruction                        A  B  C
    Children's literature                        A  B  C
    Young adult literature                       A  B  C
    Other education and library science courses  A  B  C

Other User Groups

  Campus laboratory school                       A  B  C
  Community schools ⎫
                    ⎬  Parking & access          A  B  C
  Community children⎭

Other Libraries                                  A  B  C

Audiovisual Centers                              A  B  C

Remote Access Facilities

  Listening and language laboratories            A  B  C
  Telecommunications                             A  B  C
  Computer Center                                A  B  C
```

Figure 1

kept current many outdated or superseded items will be withdrawn on a regular basis. Still, growth will occur--often
because of the addition of new services or because of new developments in elementary and secondary education. In recent
years some materials production centers have had to add new
facilities for video production. In most cases small group
rooms were inadequate and a large classroom has had to be
converted, with sound control, lights, and camera setups for
video production added. Additional space may also be needed
for new collections. This has occurred in some centers when
the children's literature collection has been transferred from
the campus laboratory school to the curriculum materials
center.

Choosing a proper location for remodeled space requires examination by a structural engineer to determine
whether the floors have been designed to hold the weight of
bookstacks. A basement location is often chosen because it
will stand the stress of the weight and also provide protection from wide variations in temperature and humidity. When
special temperature and/or humidity controls are necessary,
the basement level is often close to the support systems for
such controls and can offer the advantage of cheaper installation than other areas.

Special Needs

In developing new or remodeled space for a curriculum materials center, one potential struggle may be to convince the architect that no amount of beautiful design and
fancy extras will substitute for a functional plan. Multilevel
facilities are difficult to keep quiet, hard to monitor, make
it difficult to move materials, and often cause increased
safety problems. The director of the center may have to
convince the architect to concentrate on clerestory windows,
versatile seating, and a varied ceiling height rather than
designing wells and stairways or multi-level floors. The architect must also be convinced of the need for visibility of
services and good traffic patterns.

Access and expansion room are very important considerations. As a community service, the center needs to
have good public parking close to the building. A single
public entrance and exit can enhance security measures for
controlling the collection and provide for extended hours of
opening even if the remainder of the building is not open.

Adjacent space should offer the possibility for suitable con-
version when the need for expansion of the center arises.

In order to be sure that space is designed for maximum flexibility, all areas should be able to hold the weight
of book stacks or microform cabinets, and all areas should
have grid wiring for equipment. Walls, while necessary to
close off certain areas, should be kept to the minimum number. Partitions should be planned in such a way that they
do not create dead air spaces which may damage materials
or interfere with the dissemination of heat. If space is kept
open, with provision for adding partitions as needed, all
needs may be met. As in any library situation, carpeting
and other acoustical measures must be used. It is difficult
to provide for unforseen future technology which may present
special problems, but it has become common to plan for a
ten-year or a twenty-year period. Sometimes it is best to
accept a plan for the shorter period, keeping in mind expansion possibilities for a second ten years but ignoring detailed
planning for that period.

Lighting patterns should permit both central switch
control and separate area controls. The most flexible way
to plan for this is to have dimmer switches in several areas
so that projection equipment does not have to be permanently
confined to a single area. The standards maintained in the
past (65-75 foot candles on tables and carrels and 25-35 foot
candles in corridors and lobbies) are still desirable, but new
energy-saving efforts dictate close examination of specific
needs in different areas. The practice of what, in many
cases, was over-lighting is to be avoided. With adequate
electric service, the needs for special lighting and for special equipment can be met at the time they are used. Current recommendations are often for only 50 foot candles over
desks and reading areas, 10-15 foot candles over projectors,
and as little as one to two foot candles for opaque projectors.
If new or remodeled space is involved, it pays to provide
for future increases in power needs with proper cable and
electric grids in the floors.

Light from windows and other ambient light needs to
be controlled. Large glass wall areas are not desirable,
because of their impact on temperature control and energy
costs, and also because of losses in light and sound control
and the loss of usable wall space. Where glass areas are
desired for decorative purposes in lobbies and lounges, new
forms of glass are available whose thermal control qualities

are said to equal those of solid walls. The publications of the Illuminating Engineering Society of North America, 345 East 47th Street, New York, N.Y. 10017, provide advice on ways to meet lighting standards.

Where sound may be projected, for example in a large conference room, provision should be made for maximum sound control. This requires a hard surface for the wall near the source of the sound and a soft surface opposite, a live ceiling and a carpeted floor. Hard surface wall coverings which serve well as a background for sound projection are available and can be used in the same way as chalk board for other classroom and discussion purposes.

Plumbing will be required for the materials production area, both for a variety of paste and laminating functions and for a dark room or photographic laboratory. Even if multimedia production takes place in some other agency, at least a sink is required in the general workroom.

In an academic library, shelving and furnishings of the curriculum center are often of the standard type developed for academic libraries. In estimating shelving one needs to know the projected size of the collection and can then use the standard library estimate that each single-face 90" section should hold 150 volumes, with modifications made for the amount of oversize material in the collection. Each section is 36 inches wide with an additional three inches allowed for the end panels on each range of shelving. The depth of the shelves will vary from eight inches for a general book collection to a 12-inch shelf for much of the non-book material. Oversize picture books, reference books, spiral-bound curriculum guides, and numerous workbooks make 10- or 12-inch shelving necessary for perhaps the larger proportion of the collection--a reversal of the usual library proportion which calls for 75-85 per cent of shelving to be 8-inch. In projecting future collection size in libraries, it is customary to talk in terms of number of volumes. Because of the wide variations in sizes and types of materials in the curriculum collection, sample measurements of the existing collection should be made to determine how many volumes (or items) can actually be stored per shelf. At the same time some consideration should be given to alternatives: shelves versus cabinets, the value of compact shelving, and possible changes in form for certain classes of materials.

While the use of standard shelving makes good sense

because of the ability to add, transfer, or remove shelving to and from the central supply of the academic library system, there are also some arguments for using the curriculum materials center as a model to introduce future teachers and media specialists to the types of furnishings and arrangements more common in the school media center. This type of shelving and storage takes more space because it is generally lower in height, has fewer shelves per section, and is often designed for only one or at most a few media forms. Its advantage is that it provides a variety of storage units and work surfaces in modular components. Its disadvantage is that the materials, while stored efficiently by form, type, or size, are more difficult to retrieve than from standard shelving which allows nearly all materials to fall in their classification order. Furnishings for school media centers are designed for portability, come in sizes for pre-school children to adults, and generally permit a wide variety of arrangements for small group, large group, or individual study. Trucks and carrying trays store materials and equipment and also make it easy to gather materials for production of learning units or for group instruction. Storage containers for books, filmstrips, cassettes, periodicals, disc recordings and tapes come in a variety of forms which allow either intershelving of all media or separate sections for the various forms.

Before the needs of the curriculum center are described to the architect designing space for these purposes, a checklist of functions and services should be prepared. This list might include such items as the following, each of which could be described in detail for an architect:

Office space
Small group space
Large group space (projection room)
Equipment circulation
Equipment repair shop
Film storage
Media evaluation activities
Media production
Materials production
Video production (special lighting, soundproofing, etc.)
Audio production (soundproof rooms)

Materials circulation
Reference service
Individual reading, listening, and viewing
Materials access and storage
Library workroom
Terminal space
Shipping and receiving
Staff lounge
Exhibits
Darkroom (photolab)
Duplicating
Typing

Communicating with the Architects

In planning new or extensively remodeled space for use as a curriculum materials center, the role of the center's director and the professional staff is often very limited. Direct contact with the project's architect may be undermined by the bureaucratic structure of a university or college. The communication lines may be something like this:

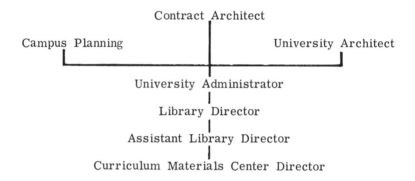

Contract Architect

Campus Planning   University Architect

University Administrator

Library Director

Assistant Library Director

Curriculum Materials Center Director

A primary element in proper planning of a curriculum center facility is communication with the architect, who should be given a description of what the center's functions are, what relationships exist externally and internally, and the quantities involved, such as numbers of people served, size of staff on duty, and sizes of collections and equipment.

Step one in designing the facility will be the translation of the center's functions into specific programs which will support these functions, and the description of space and facilities needed for each program. In many institutions this description is the only task assigned to the staff of the center and how well they communicate the needs of the programs of service to the architect will determine the success or failure of the new facility. In other institutions the director and staff of the curriculum materials center continue to be consulted from the development of the preliminary design and layout to the selection of furnishings and equipment.

In designing a facility, it is important to let the architect know the different ways in which services can be combined and to assess the desirability of contracting out some services to another campus agency if providing those services requires expensive installation of wiring, plumbing, acoustical work, and additional equipment. If an architect has been told that a remodeling project has a certain cost ceiling, it is essential that such alternatives be communicated. The architect also needs to know the relationship between circulation and reference services and professional office space; this relationship may be influenced by the personnel available. A librarian's office which is remote from the reference service area may cut down on the reference services available. Long hours of service may require that at certain times only one person will be available for both reference and circulation work.

Storage areas may also relate closely to each other. Materials for production and book repair can be grouped, for example, while repair parts for equipment may be kept in the equipment storage area. Or all of these might be grouped in one room along with the work areas associated with these items. A special area might be necessary for film storage because of heat and humidity requirements. Because of the interrelationships of the functions and the need to share similar requirements for water, electricity, telephone lines, and television and computer cables, it is desirable to analyze each service function so that functions can be grouped in different ways by their common elements.

Two samples in Figures 2 and 3 (see pp. 76-77) are representative of the kinds of forms used by campus planners in preparing the information to be given to architects hired to design new or remodeled space. In filling out such forms, activities, furnishings, and services should be described in such a way that an architect can envision just how the space is to be used. For example, Figure 2 might be completed as in Fig. 4 (see p. 78).

"Services" or "Special requirements" may include such things as water, sinks, floor coverings, drains, special electrical needs, special ventilation, telephones, special lighting, clocks, computer terminal connections, reinforced floors, gas line connections, and other items which are necessary for the functions performed in the space described. In using forms of this type it can be useful to consult books and articles on the design of libraries and media facilities. Some quantitative evaluations of the use of existing facilities can be helpful in planning, and the information can be charted for the architect's use. Figure 5 is an example of such a chart (see page 78).

ANALYSIS OF SPACE NEEDS

Descriptions of function:

Occupancy and activity performed:

Relationship to other areas:

Furnishings:

Services:

Figure 2

SPACE REQUIREMENTS

Size:

Purpose:

Maximum occupancy:

Relationship to other areas:

Special requirements (Equipment and Services):

Figure 3

ANALYSIS OF SPACE NEEDS

Description of function: Office for director's secretary.
Serves as reception area for director's office, information
point for administrative business, and working space for secretarial work.

Occupancy and activity performed: Up to four people standing before desk or seated in chairs waiting to enter director's office. One secretary seated at desk conversing with
waiting patrons or writing or typing various kinds of records
and reports.

Relationship to other areas: Immediately adjacent to director's office. Near main entrance and lobby area traffic.

Furnishings: One desk, three file cabinets, one secretarial
chair, four reception chairs, one bookcase, typewriter or
word processor.

Services: Coat closet, telephone, computer cable to central
word processor equipment, desk lamp, clock.

Figure 4

Activity	Present # of users	Projected # of users	Arrival frequency	Duration of use
Using card catalog	16	18	2/minute	8 minutes

Figure 5

This illustrates the amount of activity taking place at the
catalog in a given eight-minute period.

   After examining the descriptive forms, the architect
may combine two or more functions into one space--for
example, equipment and materials circulation may be combined, or all equipment services combined in one area. It
is, therefore, important that communication not end with the
forms submitted; the curriculum center director needs to be
able to review what the architect has done. In reviewing
tentative plans, the curriculum center staff should take time
to examine the plan carefully--perhaps assigning certain as-

pects to different people before holding a general meeting for group discussion. The person responsible for audiovisual services might, for example, be assigned to review the wiring plans, and the circulation staff might be given the task of examining proposed traffic patterns. The architect will have grouped necessary functions such as stairwells, elevators, or plumbing. These items should be examined carefully to be sure they do not interfere with normal traffic flow. Ideally, the communication should continue, architectural planners meeting with the curriculum center director and refining the relationships of functions and services. The discussions may lead to a series of compromises on such matters as whether it is more important to have circulation service near workrooms or near the office, and whether photocopy services should be near the collections or in the materials production area. The best planning system will continue to involve the center's staff in the review of architectural blueprints, sketches, or models. In this phase, mistakes must be caught--the glass wall on the staff lounge, the step that prevents the passage of book trucks, the too small elevator, the lack of soundproofing on group meeting rooms, or the lack of adequate electrical services. For these final meetings, it may be important to develop a list of questions to be asked as the review of plans takes place:

1. Are the ceilings too high or low? Either one may make uncomfortable study conditions or difficult lighting problems.
2. Are there architectural barriers that limit flexibility? Pillars or posts may make space difficult to arrange, and platforms or too many windows or doors limit the flexibility of the space.
3. Will the flow of materials be easy? It is important to be near a loading area, have elevators, and ramps instead of steps.
4. Will there be security so that the center can be open when the remainder of the building is closed? For longer hours, this may be necessary.
5. Must the center share space with some unrelated activity? This can create possible conflicts and may limit functions

Equipment Replacement

In common with many other college and university departments, curriculum materials centers usually lack a consistent plan for replacement of equipment. This can be serious in the case of audiovisual equipment, where good performance is necessary if the users are to have access to large and expensive collections of teaching materials. A study to develop a formula for equipment replacement at Purdue University Libraries and Audiovisual Center stated the problem that seems to be universal:

> Lack of provision of systematic replacement of worn out and obsolete equipment inhibits effective operational and budgetary planning in the Audio-Visual Center. [9]

While good accounting practice requires a regular program of replacement, implementation is nevertheless dependent upon funding and other considerations. At best a replacement plan has to have a great amount of flexibility built into it. Perhaps its greatest value may be in calling administration attention to the fact that continual replacement is necessary. As the authors of the Purdue study said, "In addition, this study should be forwarded to the University Business Office so that a replacement fund can be discussed and implemented in the future. "[10]

The Purdue study included estimates of the useful life of different types of equipment. [11] The actual objective of an equipment replacement plan is somewhat more general. Each piece of equipment should be examined annually in order: 1) to make an estimate of its life, 2) to compare this with other pieces of equipment to insure that replacement is made where it is most needed, and 3) to insure that a steady allotment of equipment purchases each year makes huge replacements at one time unnecessary. This insures that the budget for equipment each year, while perhaps containing some surprises or emergencies, will at least not suddenly include an impossible purchasing need. Even more important, it can prevent major interruptions in service to users of the equipment.

Physical examination of the equipment each year, together with a written record of its history, will help in planning for regular replacement needs. The records to be maintained on a piece of equipment should include information which will permit a continual reassessment of its estimated life. These data should include:

1. Identification of the piece (type, make, model,

       identification numbers)
2. Supplementary equipment dedicated to the particular piece (cover, carrying case, special microphones or earphones)
3. Identification of the supplies needed for its use (take-up reels, bulbs, cleaning supplies)
4. Record of purchase (source, cost, date of purchase)
5. Repair record (date, nature and cost of all repairs and service)
6. Service contract
7. Use schedules (occasional statistics taken for a week at a time, along with estimates of use by personnel servicing the equipment; service personnel are usually aware of which pieces of equipment are most popular and get the most use)
8. Relationship to other equipment (e.g., one of six reel tape recorders with similar functions)

The last category will aid in alerting staff when a failure of one piece of equipment might mean a total breakdown of service and a need for immediate replacement.

    It will rarely be possible to plan accurately for all contingencies. The breakdown of one very expensive piece may take the whole annual equipment budget, or the development of a new technology may require total dedication of one year's budget to a new type of equipment. In these kinds of emergencies, the plan may still help in making adjustments such as arranging for patch-up of worn-out pieces which had been scheduled for replacement. Whatever its limitations, an equipment replacement plan is still a desirable management tool and a protection against service failures.

Signs for Direction, Location and Instruction

    The sign system in the curriculum materials center should serve two functions: 1) it should offer clear directions to the primary clientele, made up of students in the college or university education programs and local teachers; and 2) it should serve as a model for signs in school media centers. As with any sign system, there is an advantage in using an architectural or design consultant.

    The purposes for signs in the curriculum materials

center are similar to those of other library areas:

1. Signs of welcome and signs which create a cheerful atmosphere
2. Directions to locations
3. Rules, regulations, and procedures
4. Services offered
5. Collection locations

If media are shelved by form, symbols could be devised for each form. The constant change in media forms and the proliferation of additional types of collections in the curriculum center are arguments in favor of signs which permit frequent change.

If the curriculum materials center is not an integral part of the general or professional education library, it may be appropriate to use signs similar to those used in a public school media center. The symbols, however, need to be more adult in nature. International system symbols can be used for restrooms, wheelchair access, or telephones, to remind student teachers that such use is one means of familiarizing children with these symbols. If diagrams and floor plans are used to show locations, they should be simple, again providing an example for the school media center, which can use such diagrams as a way to teach children how to read this type of graphic.

Bright colors and simple sans-serif lettering are suited to the atmosphere of a school media center. The practice of defining certain service areas by wall and carpet colors is too confining for a dynamic curriculum center, but a more flexible system of using signs of one color to designate a particular service or collection could be used. Bulletin boards and exhibit panels should coordinate in design with the signs. The common practice of designating major areas by signs from the ceiling may be less useful if the facility is to be used by children as well as adults.

The real value of the sign system lies always, first and foremost, in clarity and visibility. Location, proper lighting, and color contrast are the principle requirements. Standards for size in relation to distance, thickness, size and shape of letters are available from the works of designers and graphic artists. The principle common in library sign systems--flexibility for change and coordination for neatness and clarity--must also be met, but the significant difference in the curriculum materials center should be that its signs show more informality and more imagination than is usual in other academic library areas.

Conclusion

In the design, plan and arrangement of the curriculum materials center as a physical facility, many elements are similar to those of the academic library as a whole, but some significant differences make it important that this service area be considered as a separate entity. When considering existing, remodeled or new facilities, the special functions of a curriculum materials center should be the decisive factor influencing its design and arrangement.

NOTES

[1] American Association of School Librarians, Media Programs: District and School (Chicago: American Library Association, and Washington, D. C.: Association for Educational Communication and Technology, 1975).

[2] Eleanor E. Ahlers and Perry D. Morrison, "The Materials Center at the School District Level," Library Trends 16 (April, 1968): 456.

[3] AASL, Media Programs, pp. 80, 104.

[4] Harlan R. Johnson, "The Curriculum Materials Center: A Study of Policies and Practices" (ED081449) (Doctoral Dissertation, Northern Arizona University, 1973), p. 29.

[5] Cora Paul Bomar, M. Ann Heidbreder and Carol A. Nemeyer, Guide to the Development of Educational Media Selection Centers (Chicago: American Library Association, 1976).

[6] Francis L. Drag, "Curriculum Laboratories in the United States" (Doctoral Dissertation, Stanford University, 1946), p. 110.

[7] Carol Ruth St. Cyr, "Present and Potential Uses of the University of Michigan Curriculum Materials Center" (Doctoral Dissertation, University of Michigan, 1955), p. 109.

[8] Ibid., p. 111.

[9] Miriam Drake and Martha Baker, Audio-Visual Equipment Depreciation (ED112928) (West Lafayette, Indiana: Purdue University Libraries and Audio-Visual Center, 1975), p. 4.

[10] Ibid., p. 11.

[11] Ibid., p. 12.

CHAPTER 5

COLLECTION DEVELOPMENT

Developing a Policy on Selection

If a librarian is going to be able to justify the selection of certain materials and the omission of others, and maintain a collection based on rational reasons for its existence, a collection development policy is necessary. Many academic libraries require that librarians selecting materials write such a policy, which may then be modified and approved by other collection development personnel, administrators, and user groups. Before beginning the task of creating such a document, it can be instructive to examine similar documents from several sources and to study the criteria used for selection of particular types of material or subject matter.

Because instructional materials are selected by school districts and schools, a wide variety of curriculum materials selection policies is available, and some parts of them are likely to apply to an academic curriculum collection. The criteria used for selection address the particular elements important in instructional materials. State-wide policies developed as models for school districts are often useful to the curriculum materials selector in the academic library. In Florida the document, Criteria for Instructional Materials Selection, was adopted in 1975 by the State Instructional Materials Councils. It includes general criteria and special requirements for materials in language arts and mathematics. The policy addressed such issues as the expertise of the author; the scope and sequence suitability for the program; grammar and vocabulary; suitability of illustrations, charts, and maps; physical format; accuracy of content; accompanying teacher guides; skill exercises; supporting indexes, reviews, and bibliographies; stimulus for individual thinking; balanced approach in presenting women and ethnic groups; objective

85

religious content reflecting the cultural value of religions; presentation of environmental concerns; compliance with standards for publication; and legal requirements.[1]

A similar model policy produced by the Iowa State Board of Public Instruction was designed both to insure good selection and to provide a measure of protection against censorship. School districts could use it without change or as a basis for a policy adapted to local issues. This policy included statements clearly designed to avoid censorship problems. One of the criteria listed, for example, said: "Biased or slanted materials may be provided to meet specific curriculum objectives," and a statement was included on the need for a balanced collection: "The selection of materials on controversial issues will be directed toward maintaining a balanced collection representing various views."[2] The procedure for handling complaints was spelled out and sample protest forms were included.[3] The dissertation of Rollin Douma, Associate Dean for Program Development at Western Michigan University, contained a model policy which is included here in Appendix D.[4] The policy can be used as a model by schools developing their own selection policies and is also useful for the curriculum materials center staff to use in defining what they intend to collect. It is, of course, assumed that the collection in the curriculum materials center will be broader and more theoretical, with examples of materials which a school would not collect.

In general the same kinds of criteria for evaluation and selection will be used for the curriculum materials collection as appear in collection development policies for other library materials. These criteria include: 1) the expressed needs of the clientele; 2) the currency of the material; 3) its quality; 4) the relationship of the materials to the main collection and other available sources; 5) past experience with the type of material or its source; and 6) a balanced point of view. Acquisition will require the additional criteria of cost and availability.

The Expressed Needs of the Clientele

The selection of materials may be based upon certain priorities, in order to expend the usually limited materials budget to best advantage. High priority is usually given to consideration of faculty requests, library subject specialists' requests, material actually examined by the selector, or good

reviews in standard review literature.   Many materials are
selected either by traditional library acquisition methods or
by the evaluation of textbooks and other curriculum materials
and their adoption after screening by some reviewing committee or group.   Selection always involves two essentials:
knowing your clientele and learning as much as possible about
the materials.   It is not possible to be an expert in every
subject.   Selection, therefore, requires that students, community teachers, and especially the teacher education faculty
be involved in choosing materials to be purchased.

While previewing is desirable, there are complications
in the logistics of acquiring for preview, arranging a time
and place, and, hardest of all, motivating the appropriate
people to assist in this function.   The difficulties of wrapping,
shipping, and possible damage claims in returning materials
have also discouraged selectors from doing as much previewing of materials as may be desirable.   Most academic libraries, though, have approval plans which permit librarians
and other members of the academic community to examine
and return books.   In spite of the problems, some expensive
materials will have to be examined before purchase.   The
curriculum center is usually able to take advantage of the
shipping and acquisitions services in the library, but the difficulty of bringing several people together for previewing has
mostly remained an unsolved problem.   As a result much of
the previewing may be done by the curriculum librarian at
library and education association conferences.   Where a
broad clientele is available, publishers are willing and even
eager to demonstrate their materials; in some cases they
may even present them to the center after demonstration.
One beneficial function of a curriculum center, therefore, is
to sponsor and put on a media fair where all kinds of materials are displayed and demonstrated to students and local
teachers.

There are good reasons why evaluation centers are
valuable in selecting audiovisual media.   The proper procedure in studying such media forms is to start by deciding
what form might best teach a concept to a target audience.
For example, to teach the tennis serve to high school students, a filmloop might be the choice, because a short film
demonstrating the correct movements is appropriate.   The
next step would be to find out whether such a loop exists
and who sells it.   In some cases, review sources will describe and evaluate the filmloop in enough depth that the teacher would be willing to buy it without further investigation.

However, the librarian, being one step removed from the teacher, may feel that the item should be previewed by the teacher and will order it in for preview before purchase. In some cases, it might even be decided to prepare a film or video tape locally.

For good and sufficient reasons, publishers are reluctant to have some materials sent for preview. There is danger of damage or lost pieces, and the possibility that dishonest customers will make copies before returning the original. This is especially easy in audio and video tapes or cassettes. Because of its high cost of purchase, the lending for preview of 16mm film is sometimes permitted. However, the publisher often requires that a district or regional film library be the borrower rather than an individual school. Where the university center acts as a regional evaluation library, there is no problem with its serving as the agent for pre-acquisition previewing. In locations where a school district or regional center is not available or does not perform this function, the curriculum center in the local college or university might take on this responsibility for the community schools.

Teachers and librarians selecting nonbook media need to be sure that they are not designed to replace reading since children need long hours of practice in reading, and the current emphasis on basics makes reading a major focus. The bottom line in selection of nonbook media always comes back to the importance of selecting the form of media on the basis of which form best communicates the concept to the particular individual or population involved. The selector for the curriculum materials collection must always keep this in mind. Besides this major selection criterion for audiovisual materials, other basic criteria are generally the same as that for print materials. Differences usually center on the technical aspects rather than on content. Special consideration should be given to composition and focus of visual images, fidelity and synchronization of sound, and clarity of print and graphic inserts. One of the most important characteristics in audiovisual materials is the performance of the people who act or speak through the media form. Professional quality of performance is essential; without it, even the best technical efforts can give an amateurish impression.

One advantage that curriculum materials centers offer to the community is that teachers can directly examine the materials and preview an item before making a decision to purchase. For maximum effectiveness, the center needs to permit the circulation of materials. Even if the circulation period is very limited, teachers will be enabled to read or carefully examine textbooks they are considering, and audio-visual materials can be tested on sample classes.

The Currency and Quality of Materials

In the areas of currency and quality of materials, curriculum center selection policy and practice may differ from those in other parts of the library. Perhaps one of the most evident differences from the academic library collection is the large amount of material which becomes rather quickly obsolete. The pattern of textbook publishing usually requires that only the latest editions be kept in the active collection, and therefore, the ongoing process of weeding and replacement is much more important, larger in volume, and more time-consuming. Materials in the curriculum collection are useful only if they are up to date and reflect current issues and current theories of instruction. The field of education seems to be subject to quick changes in trends and practices. As a result the normal life of curricular material is seldom more than ten years, although there are exceptions to this generalization. The research needs in a college or university may make it necessary that changes in education theory and practice be documented for history of education courses. Where it is appropriate to the institution's goals, materials may be transferred to the general research collection or to special collections departments. Institutions which are members of the Center for Research Libraries will probably not keep such materials but will rely on the collections of textbooks and children's literature which CRL maintains. Many curriculum materials centers which do not regularly keep older materials may make an exception and keep Newbery and Caldecott award winners, as well as other classics of children's literature, as a permanent part of their collection.

As a general rule a children's literature collection will be weeded regularly for outdated materials, but these will not be totally replaced in the way that other materials are as new editions appear. Children's literature collections became an added responsibility of curriculum centers when some colleges discontinued the laboratory school on campus. Such schools, whether elementary or including junior and senior high, were an expensive operation and with the decline in enrollment of education students, these laboratory schools were often the first budget item to be cut. As a result, curriculum collections were sometimes expanded to include, as an added responsibility, the children's literature collection, which had been a part of the library media center for the campus school. In some cases children's literature, both fiction and non-fiction, was always part of the curriculum collection; or, in universities with a graduate library and information science program, this material was often a part of the library school collection. Even if the curriculum materials center did not collect children's literature as a research collection, some of this material was purchased as trade books. Woodbury emphasized the need for this category of material for children and young people as "particularly well suited to individualized instruction, independent study, contract learning, learning centers, innovative curriculum, and supplementary reading."[5]

Selection of materials based on quality may also present a variation in practice between the curriculum center and other library areas. Some curriculum materials librarians feel that it is important for student teachers to learn to recognize poor as well as good quality materials. For this reason they make sure that prospective teachers see and evaluate poor quality materials, so that they will learn the differences. Because reviews are widely used for some parts of the collection, such as the children's book collection, it may be important to have on hand some of the books which reviewers have judged to be poorly done. In this way the students can learn to judge material and in some cases to judge the reviewers and reviewing sources as well.

The selection of children's literature, a whole field of library specialization in itself, requires that the curriculum center professional staff become familiar with the evaluation criteria and bibliographic sources for this part of the collection. For background reading, the librarian may want to use:

Bader, Barbara. American Picturebooks from Noah's Ark to the Beast Within. New York: Macmillan, 1976.
    This historical survey of the illustrated book is a
    good overview.

Sutherland, Zena and May Hill Arbuthnot. Children and Books. Glenview, Ill.: Scott, Foresman, 1977.
    This book is used for teaching children's literature.

Rudman, Masha Kabakow. Children's Literature: An Issues

Approach. Lexington, Mass.: Heath, 1976.
Covers some of the modern concerns about the
content of children's books.

Issues in Children's Book Selection: A School Library Jour-
nal/Library Journal Anthology. New York: Bowker,
1973.
Contains articles on various aspects of collection
of children's literature.

Modern Language Association. Children's Literature: Annual of the Modern Language Association Seminar on
Children's Literature and the Children's Literature
Association. Philadelphia: Temple University Press,
annual.

Huck, Charlotte S. Children's Literature in the Elementary
School. 3rd edition. New York: Holt, Rinehart and
Winston, 1976.
Looks at children's literature from the point of
view of the teacher.

Carlson, Ruth Kearney. Emerging Humanity: Multi-Ethnic
Literature for Children and Adolescents. Dubuque,
Iowa: W. C. Brown, 1972.
Concentrates on African, Afro-American and
Mexican-American literature for children.

Useful reference tools for the selector of children's
books are:

Baskin, Barbara and Karen H. Harris. Notes for a Different Drummer: A Guide to Juvenile Fiction Portraying
the Handicapped. New York: Bowker, 1977.
Useful as a selection tool for purchasing children's
and young adult fiction dealing with the handicapped.

Writers for Young Adults: Biographies Master Index. Ed.
Adele Sarkissian. Detroit: Gale, 1979.
Indexes bibliographic and biographical information
on writers for young adults.

Yesterday's Authors of Books for Children. Ed. Anna Com-
mire. 2 vols. Detroit: Gale, 1976.
Lists authors prior to 1960.

The publishers of the Horn Book Magazine have pub-

lished four volumes on children's book illustrators, the
original Illustrators of Children's Books: 1744-1945 plus
three updates. Most librarians know that because of its
good reviews, the Horn Book is a great help in selecting
the children's book collection. If the curriculum center
has a fairly extensive collection of children's magazines,
it would be helpful to have the Subject Index to Children's
Magazines, available at 2020 University Avenue, No. 6,
Madison, Wisconsin 53705.

The Relationship of the Collection to Other Sources

Other considerations in determining priority for purchases may be whether the item is duplicated in other agencies, locational conflicts with other departments of the library, and the relationship of the item to standards and established criteria. For those academic libraries which are
members of consortia or the Center for Research Libraries,
availability of an item on loan may be another reason for
establishing a lower priority for purchase. In the acquisition process consideration has to be given as to whether it
is better to own the material or to rent or borrow it.

One important selection criterion for curriculum materials is that both local and national levels of publishing
should be represented. In some cases the local materials
will be the hardest to obtain because, for example, those
produced by a local school district may not be widely ad-
vertised, reviewed, or indexed. It is sometimes more difficult to obtain a curriculum guide from a local school or
even know that it exists than it is to get an item from a
well-organized state education department across the country.
The New York State Education Department produces a fairly
comprehensive list, although it sometimes misses some titles.
The Bureau of Curriculum Development in the State Education
Department of New York began collecting courses of study in
1940, realizing that it had to be selective rather than comprehensive, but collecting from outside the state as well as
within. At one time these items appeared in Bookmark, but
it is now reported that all of those produced in New York
are supposed to be deposited in ERIC. As is the case with
other state documents in most states, the adequacy of inter-
agency communication is not such that one can expect a list
from any state education department to be complete. When
the teacher training program places student teachers in
several school systems, it is necessary that the curriculum

materials center obtain the curriculum guides and courses of study directly from these systems. This is probably the only way to be sure that the students doing a practicum will have access to guides relevant to the school where they will teach.

At the same time, attention should be given to nationwide sources for materials, and to certain foreign or international sources. Because there are great differences in the amount of curricular material published by the various states, exchange programs with other centers in states which produce materials relevant to the local needs are important. Materials produced in California and New York State are usually well known to curriculum center librarians, but other states may do as much or produce materials more appropriate for a particular center's collection. Some curriculum materials centers produce useful guides and bibliographies which have a use broader than their immediate purpose of aiding the local clientele. For example, the Sacramento County Educational Media Center has a series of bibliographic guides with such titles as Self Esteem, Feelings on Substance Abuse, Law and Justice, Alternative Transportation, and Holidays. These can serve as useful selection tools for teachers or for other curriculum centers. They include sources, prices, and reading levels.

The selection policies for the curriculum collection need to be carefully integrated into those of the library so that no problems arise in regard to duplication or the selection of the proper location. The nature of curriculum materials, and the use which is made of them, differ in enough characteristics from traditional academic library materials and their use to require careful application and other modification from the policies and practice in the rest of the library system. Flandro reported one response to his investigation which seems quite widely accepted today: "All materials in the curriculum laboratory are to pertain to the practical application of any problem within the curriculum. No general education, methods, or theory books are to be included unless they contain a large section of practical suggestions."[6] While this statement does not apply if the curriculum collection is a part of the education library, the unique characteristics of any curriculum collection make it important that it be clearly differentiated from professional and theoretical education materials.

Flandro also concluded that "The curriculum laboratory should not be merely a professional library or a pub-

lishers' exhibit center, nor should it be a catch-all for left-
over or unclassified materials.   It should contain an up-to-
date and balanced collection of materials that have been selected to meet a variety of curriculum development needs of
classroom teachers and other pre-service and in-service
personnel responsible for the experience of children. "[7] It is
clear that the policy for accepting gifts should be as strict
as the policy for purchase of materials.   Some curriculum
centers have destroyed the integrity of their collection and
wasted space because they have permitted faculty to contribute unwanted materials or have become the dumping
ground for pamphlet or audiovisual items which other departments of the library did not want but were reluctant to dis-
card.

The wide variation in size and nature of academic
curriculum collections is justified because of the variations
in the clientele served.   This variation often depends on the
relationship of the center to other services on campus or in
the community.   One college in the California State University system, for example, is able to operate with a fairly
limited number of materials because it is located near an
education materials evaluation center run by the county board
of education.   The students may use the county center, and
the teachers in the community seldom have any reason to use
the college facilities.   In contrast, one of the colleges in the
New York State system is heavily used by educators in the
surrounding area because of its isolated rural location.   As
a result, it supplies a wide diversity of types of education
material, and is widely used by local teachers.

Past Experience with the Type of Material
and Sources for Acquisition

Arnett said in her 1965 study: "As earlier studies
showed, the most popular instructional materials in curriculum laboratories were textbooks, and their accompanying
items, courses of study, curriculum guides, and teacher
handbooks. "[8] Librarians serving in instructional materials
centers feel that this generalization is still true--an obvious
result of the demands in courses in educational methods and
curriculum design.   However, increasing emphasis on individual instruction has been reflected by an equally high
rating for supporting materials.   Because so much curriculum
material is hard to locate because of the lack of good bibliographic information, the reference services need to have as

many published bibliographies as possible, and to establish an extensive collection of publishers' catalogs as well.

Review sources are widely used for the selection of the children's literature collection, nonbook media, and some of the curriculum materials. Curriculum Review is a necessary periodical for both users and selectors of curriculum materials. Published five times a year by Curriculum Advisory Service, it arranges published curriculum materials in subject areas: mathematics, language arts, science, and social studies. It also devotes one section in each issue to articles and reviews on a specific area of current concern, such as mainstreaming, values education, or vocational education. This periodical is essential for the selector of materials for the center, since it serves both as a source of reviews and as a means of keeping up with trends in curriculum development in elementary and secondary education. Reviews are signed and are usually the work of teachers, librarians, and faculty in the field of education at the college and university level. The reviews vary in length from a few paragraphs to one-thousand word evaluative essays. While Curriculum Review claims to review all kinds of textbooks, trade books, and similar material, its weakness is the lack of enough reviews of non-commercial material and ephemeral materials which are so hard to find. The reviews include all acquisitions information including the grade level.

Other periodicals such as School Library Journal, School Media Quarterly, Booklist, and Audiovisual Instruction and Film News, which are already well known to librarians, are also widely used as review sources for all types of media. The Horn Book is used extensively for the children's literature collections. The Booklist, published by the American Library Association, has a retrospective bibliography, Books for Children, Preschool through Junior High School, which includes in annual editions the materials selected and reviewed by Booklist. Prior to 1968, it was titled Books for Children. Audiovisual Instruction has a column, "Have You Seen These?" and a "Guide to New Products" in the September issue. School Media Quarterly has articles on selection and reviews, although it does not review textbooks. School Library Journal is probably essential as a selection tool, and it also keeps the librarian up to date on what is new in school media centers and, indirectly, in the schools. Reviewers are fairly conscientious about presenting both negative and positive responses. SLJ reviews all topics although, understandably, it is heavy on literature.

Other sources for reviews include Selecting Materials
for Children and Young Adults: A Bibliography of Bibliographies and Review Sources, which leads the selector to
other review sources. Children's Book Review Index is an
annual of children's book reviews appearing in Gale's Book
Review Index, and Children's Literature Review excerpts and
cites references to criticism of children's literature.

Another tool leading the librarian to sources for curriculum materials is Education Media Yearbook. This Bowker publication should be either in the library or the curriculum materials center so that the selectors of materials
can have access to it. Its articles include both the annual
review type and those providing background for media concerns. It serves as a source book by its listings of bibliographies and catalogs of print and non-print materials. Many
items in its "Classified List" should be in the reference collection of the curriculum center, e.g., El-Hi Text Books in
Print, Audio Visual Market Place, or 101 Make and Play
Reading Games for the Intermediate Grades. The Yearbook
also identifies periodicals about media, media about media,
organizations and associations involved in media, film rental
libraries, training programs, and funding sources for grants.

The Contributions of Professional Associations

Professional associations and organizations concerned
with curriculum materials are important resources, not only
for bibliographies and lists of materials and their sources
but also for advice and information useful to the librarian
newly employed in a curriculum center. Phi Delta Kappa,
an education society with headquarters in Bloomington, Indiana, established the School Research Information Service
(SRIS) under a grant from the Kettering Foundation and publishes the SRIS Quarterly and other materials on curriculum
development. Its Fastback Series, funded by the Phi Delta
Kappa Educational Foundation, is a helpful source for learning
about many of the current and continuing important issues
that are being discussed in the field of public education.
Some titles included in the series are: Multiethnic Education:
Practices and Promises; What I've Learned About Values Education; The Uses of Standardized Testing; and Defining the
Basics of American Education. Number 110 in the Fastback
Series, Selecting Instructional Materials, is especially appropriate because of the overlap between school selection practices and what is done in the academic curriculum materials
center.

The Association for Supervision and Curriculum Development produced a pamphlet by Richard J. Miller titled Selecting New Aids to Teaching. It can be helpful in assisting students and teachers in learning to make selections. It emphasizes the procedures and policy for a school or school system, but guidelines for examining materials are also included. It is directed toward the school seeking a total unit or system for making a complete curriculum change where a large expenditure is expected. Some of the tests applied to materials might be applied to any selection decision, and certainly the whole document is important for use by curriculum committees which come to the curriculum materials center seeking advice. Examples of test questions in materials selection include:

3.2.1.5. Do the materials have student appeal?

3.2.1.6. What procedures have the producers employed for content validation?

3.3.5. Is 'hard' conclusive evidence available to indicate that learning will be improved over what is now achieved?[9]

The Education Products Information Exchange (EPIE) is a division of the Institute for Education Development, a research organization. It publishes EPIE Reports, formerly the Educational Products Report, bimonthly. Each year it produces eighteen EPIEGram--Materials issues and eighteen EPIEGram--Equipment reports designed "for improving the selection and use of instructional materials and equipment."[10] Its evaluators "are well trained in evaluating materials,"[11] and provide good reviews of materials, systems, and equipment. Besides its publications activities, the EPIE Institute offers workshops for selectors of education media of all types.

The American Association of School Librarians, an affiliate of the American Library Association, has a pamphlet, Policies and Procedures for Selection of Instructional Materials, giving some of the basic criteria for selection in schools, and produces other publications relevant to an academic curriculum collection.

In 1966, the National Information Center for Educational Media (NICEM) was established as an outgrowth of the work begun several years before at the University of Southern

California in indexing its extensive collection of films. Under
a grant from the U.S. Office of Education, the index to these
films was prepared as a computerized data bank from which
printed and microform indexes were produced. Since then
the data bases have expanded to include all kinds of media except print, and these data bases are available online through
DIALOG. In addition to the information which NICEM re-
ceives from the Library of Congress about the items for
which LC produces card sets, other items are gathered from
publishers and libraries. Input from media centers and libraries assures that many local items are covered. Included
in the printed or microform indexes are videotapes, 8mm
film cartridges, 16mm film, 35mm film, audiotapes and
discs, slides, transparencies, and filmstrips as well as indexes of publishers and distributors. NICEM also publishes
subject indexes and its Special Education Index to Learner
Materials, produced by the National Information Center for
Special Education, is useful for schools newly involved in
the mainstreaming of handicapped children into the regular
classroom.

To make maximum use of the printed indexes and bibliographies, it is necessary to maintain an organized collection of publishers' and equipment dealers' catalogs. There is
probably no substitute for browsing through such catalogs to
give the student with an education major a real feeling for
the breadth and depth of the materials, supplies, and equipment available to teachers. The materials catalogs often
give more detailed information than the listings in an index.
Students should receive some instruction in recognizing the
names of the most reputable publishers and in evaluating carefully any statements from the necessarily biased sellers of
materials. It is also important to realize that the production
center is itself a source for materials. Here again, as with
gifts from faculty, the curriculum materials selector should
not accept as a gift any materials produced in-house which
are not useful to the clientele. Those which are potentially
useful should be copied or sought as a donation. Materials
produced may include curriculum guides, units, filmstrips,
recordings, videotapes, posters, and learning centers.

A Balanced Point of View

The difficulty in obtaining curriculum materials which
present a balanced point of view seems to be increasing, with
the threat of censorship looming as a very real problem.

Student teachers need to know the facts about censorship as it applies to classroom and school media center materials. The number of censorship cases is growing and many of them result in a decision to censor materials for children and young adults. Future teachers need to know that successful attempts to censor materials in Texas have resulted in changes in certain publications. Publishers are reluctant to produce textbooks which exclude a large market such as the whole state of Texas. To avoid this type of limitation on the materials used in teaching, future teachers need to be aware of potential sources of community support for their selections and need to know in advance their own thoughts and values on the subject of censorship. The curriculum materials center should provide enough materials on censorship to assist its own selectors and its clientele in the college in arriving at their own philosophy. A brief introduction to the subject which has proven popular for the instruction of new teachers is Diane Divoky's "How to Fight Censorship." Ms. Divoky devised a set of sensible rules for building support before a censorship attack occurs. Her advice also included "Call the best lawyer," a sensible reminder that teachers, librarians, and children do have Constitutional rights. [12]

Censorship may be exercised for a number of reasons but the censorship of materials for school children is usually an outcome either of society's attempts at socializing children to its cultural standards or of the fact that children learning to read need access to a proscriptive list of materials which best suit the function. However, the topics which are often censored in children's materials do not differ greatly from the subjects attacked in censorship of adult materials. Criticism focuses largely on morality and politics. Censorship of school materials is not a new phenomenon. The teaching of evolution was a serious problem in the 1920s and still continues to be so in some locations. In the 1950s, censors were looking at the teaching of loyalty and were searching for evidences of subversion, Communist influence, or any suspect ideas which could be blamed on a Communist conspiracy.

Recent examples of textbook censorship often stem from the complaints of special interest groups. The Supreme Court ruling which left to the community the right to choose its own values is reflected in much current controversy about censorship of materials in schools. This ruling opened the door for every special interest group to try to impose the

particular views of its members on others. An example of
such a case was described in a recent article:

> In 1976, the Texas State Textbook Commission
> banned five common dictionaries that contain al-
> legedly obscene definitions--for example, a defini-
> tion of bed as a verb. The banning was prompted
> by complaints presented by Norma Gabler, who,
> with her husband, regularly submits bills of parti-
> culars on objectionable portions of textbooks being
> considered for adoption.... In a recent Sixty
> Minutes appearance, several textbook publishers
> acknowledged that they have revised some of their
> publications to insure that they will pass the
> Gablers' scrutiny. [13]

In response to a Time article about censorship activities of the Gablers, the letters to the editor were mixed;
some supported the Gablers' activities and some ridiculed
their views. [14]

This kind of reaction is indicative of how widely the
community can disagree. Given this situation a textbook
collection serving a wide community may be in the difficult
position of serving teachers from one county which approves
a set of books and also have as patrons some teachers from
the next county across a state border where the materials
are not state approved. The provision of a fairly comprehensive collection becomes a necessity if both groups are to
have access to a wide variety of materials from which to
choose. While most curriculum centers have a special relationship with the public schools of their own state, their
staffs assume that they should be serving all teachers, including those from other states or from private schools.

Censorship of children's materials differs from other
censorship efforts in that the attacks may be based on poor
quality of writing or illustration, elements which are seldom
found in censorship of adult materials. In some cases the
protest can be a legitimate attempt to protect young learners
from shoddy, banal, and tasteless material which might turn
them away from all reading. Unfortunately, this element of
quality may be easily used to justify refusal to select materials when the actual reason is controversial content.

Among the titles being censored in schools are The
Grapes of Wrath by John Steinbeck, J. D. Salinger's Catcher

in the Rye, George Orwell's 1984 and Harper Lee's To Kill
a Mockingbird, books whose quality would appear to have
been established over the years. Some critics have attacked
the classics of black literature produced in recent decades;
works by James Baldwin and Eldridge Cleaver have been censored for some of the language used. Other groups may
censor older children's books such as The Bobbsey Twins
Series, and Little Black Sambo as racist. Single issues of
periodicals are often removed because of an article considered too sexually explicit, and some periodical titles have
been condemned as a whole, usually for racial or political
reasons. Even some college textbooks have been affected.
An example of special interest group censorship of materials
is the boycott of Hoost Waldemar Janson's The History of
Art. Because it does not include a single woman artist, the
Coalition of Women's Art Organizations (CWAO) has boy-
cotted this well-known textbook which has been in common
use for almost twenty years. [15] When teachers or librarians
boycott a book, the effect is censorship imposed upon most
of their students.

A more positive approach might be to add necessary
supplementary material to counteract claimed deficiencies.
In school libraries or classrooms, censorship attacks often
come also from school administrators anxious to avoid any
sources of conflict with parents or other citizens. Schools,
therefore, should have a good set of policies on selection
and censorship so that administrators can be made aware of
the problems and make decisions only after careful consideration of the issues. In a college or university, this type of
problem is much less severe. The dedication of faculty to
intellectual freedom provides a powerful bloc of articulate
people when a censorship attack occurs. At the same time
the public has a much greater understanding of the nature of
research in higher education and even those who disapprove
will tolerate the examination of a wider variety of issues by
adults or college-age young people. There is less fear that
young people of this age will be "corrupted" by bad language
or radical political ideas.

Censorship in the materials center is more often an
indirect problem. The materials placed on deposit for
evaluation (usually textbooks and accompanying instructional
materials) may be attacked for a variety of political or
racist reasons or for presenting values not acceptable to the
community. When the center acts as a textbook evaluation
center for a state education department program, its person-

nel need to be involved in the defense of the right to read.
Academic librarians can help by marshalling the support of
the American Association of University Professors, the
American Library Association, and the Freedom to Read
Foundation. The Foundation, together with the National
Council of Teachers of English, has been involved in cases
where removal of books from approved state lists has seri-
ously interfered with the teaching of English. The "Library
Bill of Rights," approved in revised form by the American
Library Association in 1980, clearly states the duty of a librarian to become active in support of intellectual freedom
(see Appendix C).

The majority of censorship cases are subtle, for
example involving a teacher or librarian rejecting material
that is controversial, and often rationalizing the reason for
rejection as poor quality. Self-examination may be necessary to determine just what the real reason for rejection is.
In 1953, Lester Asheim defined the difference between selection and censorship and his statement is still a valuable
guide for the selector:

> Selection ... begins with a presumption in
> favor of liberty of thought; censorship, with a
> presumption in favor of thought control. Selec-
> tion's approach to the book is positive, seeking
> its value in the book as a book and in the book as
> a whole. Censorship's approach is negative, seek-
> ing for vulnerable characteristics wherever they
> can be found--anywhere within the book, or even
> outside it. Selection seeks to protect the right of
> the reader to read; censorship seeks to protect--
> not the right--but the reader himself from the
> fancied effect of his reading. The selector has
> faith in the intelligence of the reader; the censor
> has faith only in his own.
> In other words, selection is democratic while
> censorship is authoritarian, and in our democracy
> we have traditionally tended to put our trust in the
> selector rather than in the censor. [16]

The curriculum materials center personnel should
direct their best efforts toward providing information on the
development of selection policy statements which schools can
adopt. Such statements help to answer complaints and provide
a basis for any legal cases which may arise. The elements
to include in a selection policy which is designed to forestall

censorship have been identified in a doctoral dissertation by Rollin George Douma:

1. Identification of selection committee members
2. Approval of District Board of Education
3. Philosophy of selection
4. Legal authority
5. Delegation of legal authority
6. Reference aids used in selection
7. Criteria for selection
8. Procedures for handling complaints
9. Forms for complaints.[17]

The entire model policy which appears here as Appendix D is helpful to any school in defining its own philosophy as well as in preparing a formal statement.

Special Considerations for the Selector of Instructional Materials

Librarians first encountering the special needs and problems of curriculum materials collections must be aware of some considerations which affect the selection process. Some of these special considerations may not be understood by the librarian whose service in the academic library has been directed to selection in support of university course work and research.

About half of the states have official adoption procedures for instructional materials* to be used in public schools and librarians working with such materials in these states have a further complication to consider. As part of the adoption procedure, state education departments have sometimes set up evaluation centers where the materials adopted can be examined by teachers, administrators, curriculum committees, library media specialists, and the public. Whether or not the academic center is selected to act as such an evaluation center, its collection must reflect some of the results of this practice if it is to serve its clientele properly.

---

*Some materials centers define instructional materials as textbooks and materials used in the classroom, and educational materials as those in the library whose use is optional.

The state procedures are usually a two-step process, sometimes undertaken by two separate bodies, sometimes by a single group. The first step evaluates materials on the basis of state regulations and laws, and covers such elements as state purchase contracts and bidding procedures, compliance with standards for physical form such as binding or electrical standards, paper, printing, or technical photographic quality. Materials which meet all of these basic legal requirements may also then be evaluated for other legal requirements, such as their presentation of women and ethnic minorities in all types of roles, their presentation of the balance of labor and capital, their attitude on ecological concerns, health and safety education, and religious doctrine, or in some cases specific requirements for inclusion of the Declaration of Independence or the United States Constitution. After these criteria have been met, the materials thus far approved must then be evaluated in a second step by an appointed committee made up of teachers, administrators, curriculum specialists, librarians and lay members representing parents and the public. This type of committee may be a statewide body or the function may be delegated to a county or district-level group.

This group, which is made up primarily of professional educators directly involved with such materials, will then evaluate each item on a comparative form. Brought to bear upon the task will be the committee's knowledge of authors, publishers or producers, physical durability, subject content, use to the curriculum, grade and language level, quality and appropriateness of illustrations, literary quality, student interest, supporting guides and handbooks, ease of use, and costs. It is clear that before the materials ever arrive in an evaluation center where teachers and school curriculum committees can see them, much time has been taken by this bureaucratic procedure. This time period may be further extended if special groups raise objections to some of the approved materials. In such a case, hearings, special meetings, or court cases may take place. The effect on textbooks and other materials is that their publishers or producers make them more bland, stereotyped, and standardized in order that no special requirement will be missed and that no special interest group will be offended. Woodbury pointed out that this kind of evaluation and selection procedure "tends to remove small or innovative publishers from many important markets, though it produces texts that the publishers can claim reflect the expressed needs of educators."[18] Unfortunately it also reflects the needs of bureaucrats, politicians,

and special interest groups, and may in the process eliminate
the literary gem or the forerunner of a new educational in-
novation.   In some states, however, lists of state-adopted
titles are so extensive that they can be used as another selection tool by selectors in other states.   Given the restrictions of the evaluation procedure, they would have to be supplemented with other materials.

Librarians selecting for the curriculum collection
should also be aware of the common codes which publishers
and compilers of bibliographies use to designate types of materials and reading or instruction levels.   Some of the bibliographic sources for curriculum materials use the designator
codes from the Standards for Cataloging Nonprint Materials.
These are also widely used with other cataloging systems.
These codes are basically mnemonic, using F for filmstrip,
G for games, A for audiorecordings.   The general category
always adds only an A; for example, GA is the general game
designator, while GM is used for a game, GP for a puzzle
and GS for a simulation.   The selector should be familiar
with this code list in the Standards before using some of the
source indexes and bibliographies. 19   Publishers' catalogs
also often use the level of instruction abbreviations from the
Standards.   These are:

For levels	Use the term	Abbreviation
Pre-school	Pre-school	K
Grades K-3	Primary	P
Grades 4-6	Intermediate	I
Grades 7-8	Junior high	J
Grades 9-12	Senior high	H
College and adult	Adult	A[20]

Sometimes materials will be under consideration for
purchase which have not been reviewed and for which the
publisher has not supplied accurate reading level information.
Evaluating this material can be time-consuming.   If the item
is available for examination, the Fry Readability Scale can
be applied to find the reading level.   The Readability Graph
designed by Edward Fry is a quick and easy way to determine
the reading level of materials.   This scale is based on the
concept that short words and short sentences are the easiest
to read.   To use the Fry Readability Graph, three 100-word
selections are chosen from the beginning, middle and end of

the book; from these selections the total number of words in
each sentence is counted to the nearest tenth; the total number of syllables in each 100-word selection is also counted.
The three figures from each category are averaged and the
results plotted on the graph to find the reading level. Fry
ran tests against other readability formulae and found a high
correlation of accuracy for his scale.[21] The latest version
of the Fry Scale is available from Jamestown Publishers,
P. O. Box 6743, Providence, Rhode Island 02940.

Conclusion

　　The criteria for selecting curriculum materials differ from those for other library selection in several sub-
stantive ways. For this reason the professional personnel
in the curriculum materials center need to have a written
policy as well as access to basic bibliographies and reference tools which help in evaluation and locating of the materials. The scope and diversity of materials and sources demand that the selector be alert to all of the ways that curriculum materials can be obtained. While no list of selection
tools is complete and bibliographic control of learning materials is an ever-changing field, attention to basic sources
will familiarize the new professional with the agencies that
are producing good reviews and selection information.

NOTES

[1]Criteria for Instructional Materials Selection, 1975 Adoption
　　(ED 101 753) (Tallahassee: Florida State Department
　　of Education, 1975).

[2]Jean Dornfield, ed., Selection of Instructional Materials;
　　a Model Policy and Rules (ED 116 691) (Des Moines:
　　Iowa State Department of Public Instruction, 1975),
　　p. 7.

[3]Ibid., pp. 8-17.

[4]Rollin George Douma, "Book Selection Policies, Book Com-
　　plaint Policies, and Censorship in Selected Michigan
　　Public High Schools" (Doctoral Dissertation, Universi-
　　ty of Michigan, 1973), pp. 120-141.

[5]Marda Woodbury, Selecting Instructional Materials, Fast-

back Series no. 10 (Bloomington, Indiana: Phi Delta Kappa, 1978), p. 17.

[6]Royce P. Flandro, "Curriculum Laboratories in Colleges of Teacher Education" (Doctoral Dissertation, Indiana University, 1957), p. 113.

[7]Ibid., p. 193.

[8]Helen Mae Arnett, "Accessibility of Instructional Materials with Implications for the Organization of Curriculum Laboratories" (Doctoral Dissertation, Western Reserve University, 1965), p. 155.

[9]Richard I. Miller, Selecting New Aids to Teaching (Washington, D.C.: Association for Supervision and Curriculum Development, 1971), p. 10.

[10]"EPIE: Educational Products Information Exchange," Audiovisual Instruction 12 (April, 1967): 383.

[11]Woodbury, Selecting Instructional Materials, p. 11.

[12]Diane Divoky, "How to Fight Censorship," Learning: The Magazine for Creative Thinking 3 (August-September, 1974): 40-45.

[13]Dorothy C. Massie, "Censorship in the Schools: Something Old and Something New," Today's Education 69 (November-December, 1980): 6.

[14]"Letters: Textbook Censors," Time 115 (January 28, 1980): 6.

[15]"Boycott Called on Sexist Texts," On Campus with Women 26 (Spring, 1980): 16.

[16]Lester Asheim, "Not Censorship but Selection," Wilson Library Bulletin 28 (September, 1953): 67.

[17]Douma, Book Selection Policies, pp. 123-141.

[18]Woodbury, Selecting Instructional Materials, p. 8.

[19]Alma M. Tillin and William J. Quinly, Standards for Cataloging Nonprint Materials. 4th ed. (Washington, D.C.: Association for Educational Communications and Technology, 1976), pp. 26-28.

[20]Ibid., p. 21.

[21]Edward Fry, "A Readability Formula That Saves Time," Journal of Reading 11 (April, 1968): 513-518.

CHAPTER 6

ACQUIRING THE MATERIALS

The Acquisitions Role of the Curriculum Materials Center

Many of the dissertations on the curriculum materials center end with a conclusion that the provision of teaching materials is the essential function of these centers in the academic library setting. The provision of materials requires that the processes of evaluation, selection, solicitation and production will be primarily the responsibility of the professional staff of the center. As a general rule the operations of searching, ordering, accounting, and receiving of materials from publishers and vendors will be done by the acquisitions departments of the library system, and these technical service areas will control the flow of monographs and serials into the collection. However, the nature of the sources for some of the curriculum collection means that some parts of the acquisition function may not be handled by the technical services personnel in the general library system. The acquisition of materials purchased from commercial vendors can be handled in a way similar to all other library materials, but the solicitation and production of some materials may have to be handled by the staff of the curriculum center. The differences in procedures will be especially apparent in handling such items as curriculum guides, courses of study, samples of educational programs, community resources information, display materials, free materials, and those which result from in-house production.

In the academic library, the actual preparation of orders and communication with vendors and publishers as well as the handling of the financial records of the operation and the checking in of materials as they are received is usually done by the department or departments responsible for all library acquisitions. Some exceptions to these procedures may occur where many gift items of an ephemeral nature are acquired or where there is extensive use of free materials. Some libraries, however, accept all incoming items in the acquisitions areas in order that good statistics on the size of the collection can be kept in a single location.

The government publications department may be the closest example of a library unit which shares some responsibility for acquisitions in the same way as curriculum materials centers. In some libraries the government publications personnel may spend considerable time in acquisition and checking in of materials, many of which are free under the government publications depository system. Because some libraries purchase part of the government publications collection and receive part of it free, only those materials which require a financial transaction may go through the acquisitions department or a serials acquisition unit. Where only part of the collection is cataloged, this may also be handled by the general technical services personnel, while the bulk of the collection, received on deposit without charge, is often completely the responsibility of the government publications department or unit.

In curriculum materials centers the procedures also vary. Some centers handle all of their own acquisitions functions except for those involving financial accounting; some centers place orders for certain kinds of materials through the use of personal contacts and form letters, with the receiving done in the technical services areas; some centers expect the acquisitions departments to place all requests, for free materials as well as for those purchased, and expect the library's gifts and exchange section to handle such materials. Another set of procedures may be used where the curriculum materials center serves as an official evaluation center for the state or county education department. In this case the center may accept materials for current evaluation and only route them through the acquisitions department when they have been selected to become part of the more permanent collection and be cataloged as part of the library's inventory. The decision on whether or not materials will be entirely handled by the library's acquisitions units is usually based on whether the technical service departments have full responsibility for statistical records on the library's collection, whether the materials are free or purchased, and whether or not the items received are to be cataloged.

Free Materials

When curriculum materials centers were first developed, much of the material they acquired was free. Developed in colleges or departments of education, these centers usually had little money for materials, and publishers
eager to reach the nation's future teachers were liberal with
gifts of textbooks and teachers' manuals. Curriculum guides
were collected from local schools, developed by education
professors, or collected at professional education meetings.

While the era of the free collection is gone, some
curriculum materials are still available from free and inexpensive sources to a greater extent than is true of the other
collections of the general library. Publishers of textbooks
are still fairly generous with donations to the academic centers. Often the decision as to whether or not such a donation is to be made seems to be the responsibility of the local
sales force; as a result there seem to be wide variations
in practice. Publishers of children's encyclopedias are often
willing to deposit the latest edition of their sets, either on
loan or as a gift, and tests are sometimes acquired free in
cases where a publisher is willing to deposit a sample for
teaching purposes. A wide variety of materials is likely to
be received free from publishers if the center is designated
as an evaluation center by a state education department or a
large school district. Curriculum guides may be free from
local sources. Model teaching units and lesson plans can be
collected from methods classes, and nonprint media developed
by students may be duplicated for the center's collection.

As long ago as 1959 Flandro pointed out that publishers were beginning to be reluctant to deposit free textbooks:

> Even though they seemed most anxious to make
> their publications accessible to potential users, they
> indicated that costs were forcing them to be se-
> lective and to deposit materials in only the more
> strategically located curriculum laboratories.[1]

Obviously the professional approach to seeking free copies of
trade books, instructional media, and textbooks from commercial publishers should be on the basis of equal mutual advantage. If the publisher is to reap an advantage from depositing a free item, it is necessary that this item be brought
to the attention of administrators, teachers, and future teachers so that multiple copies of the item are purchased for use

in schools. The publisher should know what efforts the curriculum center will make toward this goal. Some specific
practices should be adopted and the results communicated
back to the publisher or the publisher's representative.
These might include:

1. New materials from a single publisher or a
   small group of publishers may be used to form
   a special display in a prominent area of the
   center
2. Displays in the curriculum materials center or
   in conference areas may be set up for meetings
   and conferences of teachers and school media
   specialists, and these displays would feature
   the publisher's product
3. The publisher's products will be shelved with
   all other materials aimed at the subject and
   level involved. In this way people seeking any
   materials for the grade and subject will not
   fail to see the contribution the particular publisher makes to such a purpose
4. The publisher's product will be listed in bibliographies and lists distributed by the curriculum materials center both to its users and to
   local schools
5. The curriculum materials center will attempt
   to get users' evaluations of the item and for-
   ward copies to the publishing company so that
   it can improve the product
6. The publisher's representative could be invited
   to view any special efforts which include the
   product
7. Individual letters and contacts with salesmen
   are probably a better way to obtain free materials than the standard form letter which was
   a practice in the past
8. Some free materials could be obtained by regularly contacting faculty to secure sample materials sent to them.

When asking for new material as a gift from the publisher,
it is a good idea to mention the date or edition of the material now being used in the center. It has also been suggested that when sample books sent to faculty are passed on
to the center, the librarian should acknowledge this gift in
the same way as those items donated directly to the center. [2]
Curriculum materials professional personnel should also take

advantage of conferences and meetings to establish liaison with sales people at exhibit areas.

The relatively temporary nature of curriculum materials in general makes it desirable to take maximum advantage of free and low cost materials, not only to provide information on the most recent topics of interest, but because teachers may need many supplementary recent items to update a three- or four-year-old required textbook. Efficient procedures for ordering need to be worked out, however, if the costs in personnel time are not to be greater than the benefits of the free materials.

Because many free materials are a form of propaganda for the agency giving them away, the message may need to be interpreted to education students. Ideally, such materials should be selected to offer all points of view. For example, materials produced by oil companies, environmental groups, and governmental agencies might supply a balanced picture on the energy problems of this country. The staff of the curriculum center should point out this aspect of free materials to student teachers using these items.

A source for free materials is the series of Educator's Guides published by Educator's Progress Service, Randolph, Wisconsin. These include such titles as:

Educator's Guide to Free Audio and Video Materials
Educator's Guide to Free Films
Educator's Guide to Free Filmstrips
Educator's Guide to Free Guidance Material
Educator's Guide to Free Health and Recreation
    Materials
Educator's Guide to Free Science Materials
Educator's Guide to Free Social Studies Materials
Educator's Guide to Free Teaching Aids

These guides are indexed by title, subject, source, and availability, including availability in Australia and Canada. Several pages of instructional material appear in the front of each Guide to help teachers use it effectively. Proper request procedures, a sample letter of request, and criteria for selection help to insure success in acquiring the free materials listed in each Guide.

The Elementary Teacher's Guide to Free Curriculum Materials (Cover title: Educator's Guide to Free Curriculum

Materials) does not usually include such things as curriculum guides from school districts or state education departments, but it does include items from other state agencies such as state tourist departments. Included also are materials from the public service departments of business and industries, from federal agencies such as the U.S. Forestry Service, and from business and professional associations. The items listed are usually well annotated to make selection easier and each annual edition contains about 50 percent new material as well as many new sources. These Guides are valuable both as selection sources for the center and for use by teachers and students using the center.

Government Sources

One important source for free and inexpensive materials is the United States Government. While many academic librarians are already familiar with government publications, the curriculum center's staff has a duty to make student teachers and school teachers more aware of this form of information. Such books as U.S. Government Publications for the School Media Center, by Alice J. Wittig, should be in the reference collection to serve as an instruction manual and a bibliography of titles for use in the classroom or school media center. This book gives a quick rundown on the Government Printing Office, the national depository system, and the methods of obtaining and using government publications. It suggests a basic reference list of titles, lists bibliographies available and the names and addresses of the GPO bookstores. The major portion of the book's content is devoted to a selected bibliography of government publications suitable for a school media center or for classroom use. The citations are by subject categories, but a title index is also provided. Besides the advantage of having such books available as selection tools for teachers and education students, the curriculum center personnel should also use books of this type as selection tools in order to keep a reasonable number of government publications in the center's collection.

The GPO also offers curriculum guides which some centers might need, e.g., Teaching Creative Writing or A Guide to Teaching Poison Prevention in Kindergartens and Primary Grades. It is also a source for short treatises on many subjects in booklet form which would be useful to certain high school curricula. Indians of Arizona, Our American Coins, or Guia Para Comer Mejor (A Daily Guide to Good

Nutrition) are examples. All of the above pamphlets are under two dollars in price. [3]

The university or college library should have the Monthly Catalog of U. S. Government Publications Research in Education and its semi-annual indexes, a collection of ERIC documents, and other reference materials such as Education Directory, Public School Systems. Students can be referred to the library areas where these items are kept.

Bibliographic Sources

The wide variety and number of sources for selection of curriculum materials and the related materials for children raises the question of whether an extensive group of selection tools should be maintained in the curriculum materials center, or whether such material should be in the general or education reference section of the library. The nature and extent of the bibliographic source material may mean that sheer volume will dictate that the curriculum center cannot store or maintain such a collection. Also, many of the useful reference tools are useful for the college curriculum and other general purposes. Other considerations may influence the decision. If, for example, the curriculum collection is not open or does not provide professional reference service for long hours, it may be desirable that most bibliographies be kept in the general reference area where experienced people are on hand to assist community teachers and education students with problems of description and publishing information.

Large library publishers supply many of the important reference and resource books needed when selecting for curriculum development. These include such items as:

Seltz-Petrash, Ann and Kathryn Wolff, eds. AAAS Science Film Catalog. New York: Bowker, 1975.

Audiovisual Market Place 1980: A Multimedia Guide. 10th ed. New York: Bowker, 1980.
Includes sources for hardware and software, lists of AV newsletters, a calendar of events and a bibliography of reference works.

Gillespie, John T. and Christine B. Gilbert, eds. Best Books for Children: Preschool Through the Middle Grades. New York: Bowker, 1978.

Baskin, Barbara H. and Karen H. Harris. Books for the
Gifted Child. New York: Bowker, 1981.
Prepublication announcements indicate that this
book discusses the selection of books for gifted
children and includes a list of annotated titles.

Bernstein, Joanne E. Books to Help Children Cope with
Separation and Loss. New York: Bowker, 1977.
Provides lists of books within categories such as
death, divorce, and adoption.

American Crafts Council. Contemporary Crafts Market Place,
1977-78. New York: Bowker, 1977.
A source for some of the hard-to-find materials
needed in the production center.

Two basic bibliographies which should definitely be
placed in the reference collection of the curriculum center
itself are:

>Brown, Lucy Gregor and Betty McDavid, eds.
>Core Media Collection for Elementary Schools.
>New York: Bowker, 1979.

>Brown, Lucy Gregor, ed. Core Media Collection
>for Secondary Schools. New York: Bowker,
>1979.

Each of these books contains more than 3000 nonbook items,
the first for grades K-8 and the second for grades 8-12.
These books do not pretend to be anything but selection lists
and they include only titles which meet the editors' criteria--
those which have been "favorably reviewed, are award winners, or have been evaluated for their authenticity, technical
quality, student level interest, and motivation, accuracy in
content, and validity in treatment."[4] The authors have
cautioned that the books should not replace careful professional selection by the teacher or librarian who will use the
materials. However, they are particularly valuable for the
librarian just beginning to select for the curriculum collection
or for evaluating the collection. Arrangement is by subject,
but a title index is also included. Entries for each item come
under a subject such as "Art, Medieval, " "Glaciers" or
"Mozart, Wolfgang, " with a full description under one of the
subjects handled. Subject headings are from Sears' List of
Subject Headings. Each entry includes title, media form,
publishing or distribution source, date, series (if appropriate),

collation, ordering information, grade level, reviewing source, and Dewey classification number. The entry includes a list of the contents to assist the buyer who may want only part of a series or kit, and provides a brief but very useful annotation. A second edition encourages the belief that the publisher will keep these reference tools up to date.

is:
Another title which might be in the center's collection

El-Hi Textbooks in Print, 1980, 11th ed. New York: Bowker, 1980.
This contains titles of about 35,000 textbooks. It includes a series index of publishers' series and a list of publishers as well as all ordering information.

Other titles from library publishers are:

Children's Catalog. Newark, N.J.: Bro-Dart, annual.

Glendening, Corinne P., and Ruth A. Davies. Creating Programs for the Gifted: A Guide to Teachers, Librarians and Students. New York: Bowker, 1980.

Educational Film Locator of the Consortium of the University Film Centers and R. R. Bowker Company. CUFC Data Base Committee and R. R. Bowker Company Serials, Bibliography and Standards Department, ed. 2nd ed. New York: Bowker, 1980.
This is a union catalog of the film libraries of CUFC members and a source of film rentals on 40,000 films.

Richardson, Selma K. Periodicals for School Media Programs. Chicago: American Library Association, 1978.

The Elementary School Library Collection: A Guide to Books and Other Media. Lois Winkel, ed. Williamsport, Pa.: Bro-Dart Foundation, 1979.

The Education Film Library Association offers a variety of publications at a discount to its members but available also to others. These publications include sources for films such as:

> University and College Film Collection, 3rd ed.
> Bloomington, Indiana: Indiana University
> AV Center, 1974.

and how-to-do-it help such as:

> Jones, Emily S. Manual on Film Evaluation, rev.
> ed.

and numerous film listings, usually annotated and evaluated and costing only a dollar or two. The association's address is 43 West 61st Street, New York, N.Y. 10023.

A great variety of less well known publishers produce valuable source bibliographies and resource materials. Examples are:

> Best Buys in Print. Ann Arbor, Mich.: Pierian
> Press. Quarterly.
> Hendershot, Carl. Programmed Learning: A
> Bibliography of Programs and Presentation De-
> vices, 3rd ed. Bay City, Mich.: The Author,
> 1965.
> New York Graphic Society. Fine Art Reproductions.
> Greenwich, Conn.: New York Graphic Society,
> 1978.
> Shaffer, Dale E. Sources of Free Teaching Mate-
> rials. Salem, Ohio: D. E. Shaffer, 1975.

and Video Users Market Place, a periodical from Knowledge Industries, 2 Corporate Park Drive, White Plains, New York 10604.

One of the services of the curriculum materials center is to make beginning teachers aware of sources of information at the Library of Congress and other agencies of the federal government. The National Audiovisual Center, a part of the National Archives and Records Service under the General Services Administration, Washington, D.C. 20409, has a reference section which responds to mail or telephone inquiries and has a computerized data file for identifying films in its collection. It attempts to find sources for loans of federally produced films which have no rental fees, and can also provide lists and catalogs of audiovisual materials for sale in twenty-one different subject categories.

Finding and Acquiring Curriculum Guides

Federal sources are also helpful in acquiring curriculum guides. Through the ERIC system, the federal government is a major source of education materials, some of which are useful curriculum items. This is especially true for the elusive curriculum guides and courses of study which are always so time-consuming to collect. Two previous sources for these materials, Education Index and Educational Leadership, no longer include much on non-commercial guides. Educational Leadership, the journal of the Association for Supervision and Curriculum Development (ASCD), used to have a regular column listing non-commercial guides. This was replaced by the association's annual publication, Curriculum Materials. Since its content is mainly a list of the guides displayed at the ASCD annual meeting, the same list may be available in the indexes of the KTO microfiche collection. Professional journals in education are a good source for some of the curriculum guides, and they can be especially valuable if the guides are actually reviewed. Curriculum guides should be evaluated with the same care as other curriculum aids. While style, format, and physical form may be inferior, the same strict criteria for accuracy, appropriateness and coordination with grade level, and recognition of the principles of good teaching, should be used.

Another federal source for curriculum guides is The Monthly Checklist of State Publications. If a state education department produces a journal or a newsletter, The Checklist often lists this publication as well as those of the state's school systems. The Monthly Checklist of State Publications is put out by the Exchange and Gift Division, Processing Service of the Library of Congress. Courses of study may be found under each state education agency, such as:

State of Texas, Education Agency, Division of Curriculum Development, Science Section. Science Framework, Kindergarten through Grade 12.

or curriculum guides such as:

State of Texas, Education Agency, Division of Curriculum Development, Social Science Section. A Comprehensive View of Brazil.

Curriculum guides may come from some agency other than the education department:

> State of Texas, Parks and Wildlife Department.
> The Ten Commandments of Shooting Safety. [5]

In some cases very complete ordering information is included in an entry:

> California State Department of Education. Taking
> Risks; Activities and Materials for Teaching
> About Alcohol, Drugs and Traffic Safety.
> Book 1, Elementary Edition; Book 2, Secondary
> Edition. Available from the Publications De-
> partment, Sacramento. $2.00. [6]

While many guides and courses of study may be listed in The Monthly Checklist of State Publications, it is often ad-visable for the center to write to the agencies mentioned and request their catalogs or price lists. Out-of-print items may be available from the Center of Research Libraries (to libra-ries which are members of CRL), since it has an extensive collection of state publications.

A curriculum materials librarian may have difficulty deciding upon purchase of an expensive set of curriculum guides such as those published in microfiche by Fearon-Pitman and KTO when many of these items may already be available in ERIC. The term "curriculum guide" will turn up many of these in an online automated search but will not, of course, identify the overlap with the Fearon-Pitman and KTO sets without a time-consuming match up of titles. The choice be-tween the Fearon-Pitman Curriculum Development Library (Fearon Reference Systems Division of Pitman Learning, Inc., 6 Davis Drive, Belmont, California 94002) and the KTO Cur-riculum Guides (Kraus Microform, Rte. 101, Millwood, New York 10546) is also difficult, although many librarians prefer the Fearon set because of its abstracts and evaluations. The cost of these relatively expensive sets should be weighed against the time and expense involved in collecting these docu-ments individually and the savings in storage space and hand-ling time. Good indexing is another major factor since it avoids the expense of individual cataloging of all guides and assists the patron in using the set with fewer instructions.

The Fearon-Pitman Curriculum Development Library includes the annual sets since 1978. The 1979 set includes 905 guides and an index set of six volumes; the 1979 set in-cludes 800 guides and seven index volumes. A cumulative index for both years is also available. The microfiche are divided into twenty-one major subject areas, such as science, mathematics, consumer education, and special education. The index volumes cover one or more of these subjects, so that a group of the microfiche can be grouped with its index. Cross-listing is done and key-word and abstract entries help in locating a guide.

The KTO set, Curriculum Development in Microfiche: Selecting Curriculum Guides, has been published each year since 1970 and is produced as a result of filming the exhibit of curriculum guides at the annual conference of ASCD. Each year's set stresses a theme: for 1977, Orchestrating Our Third Century Curriculum; for 1978, Emerging Values and Competencies; and for 1979, Assuring Quality through Equality. The guides are grouped by subject and can be purchased as a complete set, a subject group or an individual guide. General subjects like mathematics are broken down by grade level: preschool and kindergarten, elementary, middle, and secondary. Special education is subdivided into emotionally disturbed, gifted, and mentally handicapped.

Another microfiche set which includes the curriculum guides produced in the state of California is available from the San Mateo Office of Education, Curriculum Materials Depository. These have a cumulative retrospective index in Educational Resources Guide from the World of Education: Curriculum Guides 1974-80. This service has recently been discontinued and all California guides are now to be deposited in ERIC instead, just as those of New York State are already reported to be handled. Some grave doubts have been expressed that all guides will be submitted or that the collection will be as comprehensive as when the San Mateo Resource Center provided the service. Another retrospective set of guides was produced by Xerox University Microfilms (University Microfilms International) in 1974. This was indexed by subject, title and source, and included abstracts and annotations. If an increasing number of states require that courses of study and curriculum guides be deposited in ERIC, this may prove to be the single best source for such material.

For purchasing children's literature, the curriculum librarian may want to be sure that the library has the Bulletin of the Center for Children's Books, a bibliographic periodical from the University of Chicago Press. The University of Chicago has an outstanding collection of children's books and is thus a fairly comprehensive source. Another useful list is <u>Paperbound Books for Young People: from Kindergarten through Grade 12</u> (2nd edition, New York: Bowker, 1980). This contains ordering information for fifteen thousand children's paperback titles.

Conclusion

Because of the wide variety of small, non-standard publishers and the need to locate free and inexpensive materials from a variety of producers, the curriculum materials center will always need to supplement the acquisitions services provided by the library's purchasing departments.

NOTES

[1] Royce P. Flandro, "Curriculum Laboratories in Colleges of Teacher Education" (Doctoral Dissertation, Indiana University, 1957), p. 169.

[2] Harold F. Smith and Charles Gardner, "Curriculum Materials in the Teachers College Library," <u>College and Research Libraries</u> 17 (July, 1956): 313.

[3] Alice J. Wittig, <u>U.S. Government Publications for the School Media Center</u> (Littleton, Colo.: Libraries Unlimited, 1979).

[4] Lucy Gregor Brown, ed. <u>Core Media Collection for Secondary Schools</u> (New York: Bowker, 1979), p. viii.

[5] <u>Monthly Checklist of State Publications</u> 71 (Nov., 1980): 966.

[6] <u>Ibid.</u>, p. 903.

CHAPTER 7

ORGANIZING THE MATERIALS FOR RETRIEVAL

Special Cataloging Needs

The catalog for the curriculum materials center is usually still in the form of a card catalog and may either be devised exclusively for the center, be the same as that for the general library, or be a modification of the library's system. There are differences of opinion as to whether or not curriculum materials should receive full cataloging, since collections are relatively temporary: most materials have a useful life of only five to ten years. Many curriculum materials centers use only brief cataloging, usually with a non-standard classification system.

The argument against brief cataloging is that full cataloging encourages use of the materials. A standard system of cataloging makes self-service easier, makes user instruction more consistent for both the center and the remainder of the library's collections, and shortens the training program for staff. A variety of entries makes it easier for users of the catalog to find sources for needed information.

If the curriculum materials center is not to be a "stepchild" of the library, all cataloged materials should also be in the main card catalog and in any other bibliographic records which describe the library's holdings. They should thus be available to anyone on campus, subject to the necessary limitations on circulation which are found in many kinds of library collections. There are some arguments about the use of a "juvenile" note or some such designation in the call number area of the catalog card. While college faculty and students may be annoyed by being led from the main catalog to a juvenile book, in some cases such books prove to be useful because of their good illustrations and

123

simple but valuable charts and diagrams. In many cases the location symbol may be enough to alert users that the materials are apt to be at a low grade level.

Some curriculum materials centers have published materials cataloged by technical services; others do all of their own cataloging. Both practices are common and backlogs in processing are sometimes a problem in either situation. Where most of the processing is done in the center, more staff is usually available--often a second professional or high-level subprofessional and more full-time clerical positions. Some of the weaknesses that occur when cataloging is not done by the major standard systems result from the fact that processing is done in a public service unit rather than under the control of a technical services staff whose primary focus is on the organization of materials. The weaknesses of a non-standard system may include: 1) that it does not bring together all (or as much as possible) of the materials on one subject, 2) that media do not get handled in the same way and thus get shunted aside, and 3) that such efficient tools as OCLC are not used. A non-standard record can thus make it impossible to participate in the creation of a national data base and its use for inter-library loans. MacVean found that when cataloging was not done by technical processing personnel, the lacks included: "Omission of imprint, collation, notes, and certain added entries. Another limitation is the research which is done on names, dates, and editions."[1]

Some of the reasons for having cataloging done by the library's cataloging department are:

1) This area has many paraprofessional and clerical staff members who are trained in the various tasks which are part of the cataloging function

2) Various tasks are specialized, which increases efficiency

3) Necessary equipment is available, such as OCLC or RLIN terminals, labeling equipment, photocopiers, and typewriters with special keyboards

4) Bibliographic tools are available for locating cataloging copy either online or in national or special bibliographies

5) When cataloging is done here, it usually is done by a standard system and conforms to

other library collections
6) The curriculum collection usually has a set of
cards in the main library public catalog
7) Personnel in the curriculum materials center
can concentrate on public services

The marking and preparation for shelving of curriculum materials is often more complicated than for other types
of materials. At least some of the materials will need a
larger and more complex label (sometimes a tag) showing
form of material and grade level as part of the call number.
Many items come in several pieces, each of which needs to
be marked in addition to the box in which they are stored.
Where there is a high proportion of pamphlets and paperbacks, more binding or temporary binding is required. The
original boxes in which some materials are sold may not be
satisfactory for shelving. Small items may need to be in
boxes as close as possible in size and shape to books, so
that they fit well on standard shelving. Kits and games often
need a stronger box than the original. These requirements,
plus the normal insertion of security devices and bar-code
labels, make this function more suitable for the trained
marking staff in a technical service area.

The systems of classifying and cataloging materials
for the curriculum collection ought to provide for the special
needs of this type of material and:

1. Include an identification for form, grade level,
and subject, and indicate whether it is a state-
adopted item
2. Include an entry for the publisher or producer
3. Include an evaluation note in some cases
4. Put emphasis on series
5. Be a finding tool rather than a bibliographic
description
6. Bring subjects together, series together and
publishers' or producers' work together.

Cox felt that there should be two sections of the card cata-
log--one for print and another for nonprint media--because
the user seeks print "suggestions" first and "devices"
second.[2] While this does seem to be a common practice,
users can probably best be served by finding all of the materials relevant to their subject search in one area of the catalog.

The Dewey Decimal or Library of Congress classification systems, as well as some other systems, allow for subject and subdivision indexing. The problem of using the
standard DDC and LC systems is that materials which should
be in broad subject groups are in narrow subject areas, and
the subjects do not necessarily coincide with the subject
areas for elementary and secondary instruction. It is
generally agreed that there are advantages in modifying whatever system is used by not breaking subjects down to specific
detail. Classifying by the general instructional topics keeps
together all materials useful for one school subject.

One reason for choosing a certain classification and
cataloging system is the consideration of coordination with
other library collections. As Arnett said: "The Education
Librarians reported their biggest problem was coordinating
the resources of the Education Library, the Curriculum Materials Laboratory, and the University School Library."[3]
Where a school media specialist program exists, the materials may need to be cataloged in the Dewey Decimal Classification to conform with the practice in most schools. This
will insure that the future media specialists have an opportunity to observe the curriculum materials center as a model
for a school media center. Any modifications suitable for
school collections might also be used, such as abbreviated
Cutter numbers or notations for biography or short stories.
Before making this kind of decision, however, a careful
analysis should be made to see how this would affect the
useful grouping of materials for the pre-teacher population.

Johnson found Dewey the most widely used classification system, with the Library of Congress system second in
popularity. Other popular systems were the U. S. Office of
Education system, the Textbooks in Print subject headings,
and local alphanumeric systems.[4] Arrangements by subject
broken down by grade level were most popular, but grade
level divided by subject is also used. For the general curriculum collection, Bomar recommended Dewey in educational
media evaluation and selection centers and saw the basic
need to be for entries under author, title, subject, format,
and producer/publisher.[5] MacVean's dissertation indicated
that the classification schemes most used in curriculum centers, in order of frequency, were: "(1) special classification schemes without a notation, (2) the Dewey Decimal
Classification system, and (3) special classifications with a
notation."[6] This pattern which MacVean's research found
does seem to be the prevailing pattern where the processing

is done within the center. Johnson's study of the UCLA
Curriculum Inquiry Center indicated that the staff there felt
that Dewey was not satisfactory, although they have been
using a modified form of Dewey. [7]

It is generally assumed that most curriculum materials require the following elements:

1. Subject classification
2. Individual identifier--this Cutter number may
   include either publisher or author or both as
   appropriate
3. Illustrator entry where appropriate
4. Grade level
5. Date and place of publication
6. Publisher or producer entry
7. Series entry
8. Form designation
9. State textbook adoption notation
10. Author or editor entry
11. Title entry.

It may also be necessary to have both a complete shelf list
of all call numbers and another shelf list by form for nonprint media. It is generally agreed that the card catalog's
main function is to bring together subjects, series, publishers' or producers' work, and, where appropriate, authors
and illustrators.

The main reason for a series catalog is to handle
publishers' series. A separate publishers catalog subdivided
by series is probably effective since some people request
material by the series title and others by the publisher's
name. However, both entries can appear in the general catalog for the center. Publishers' representatives are reported
to be more generous with free gifts if they can be shown that
users have direct access to the materials they have donated.
Johnson reported that the reason for a publishers catalog is
that students ask for materials in this way. [8] Some centers
feel that textbooks only need a publishers catalog, and do
not require an entry for author, title, or subject, but this
is not usually considered adequate. Whether or not to have
a separate publishers catalog probably depends on how much
extra work is involved. If it is only a matter of profiling
for one extra card from OCLC, it would seem worthwhile to
maintain one, either separately or by providing an integrated
entry in the public catalog. MacVean found one center, how-

ever, that discontinued its publishers catalog because of
lack of use. [9]

Gallinger, in writing about the processing of nonprint
materials in evaluation and selection centers, made a statement which is applicable to academic library curriculum materials centers:

> Without full and accurate cataloging, following
> nationally accepted standards, storage and use of
> non-print materials in any center or library cannot
> realize its full potential.... [They] must rely on
> Library of Congress leadership, follow MARC for-
> mat and produce data compatible in every respect
> with existing library computer storage and re-
> trieval networks, especially Ohio College Library
> Center (OCLC).... If any thoughts of unique
> standards or cataloging rules exist, or operating
> as an entity completely independent of the Library
> of Congress, let them be immediately abandoned. [10]

In-house Processing

All curriculum materials centers seem to do some
processing in house. Test files, picture files, curriculum
guides and pamphlet files are usually handled by the center's
personnel. Only on such small collections can a simple system be adequate, and there are good reasons to use a fairly
simple classification scheme for materials which have a short
life. This principle is reflected in centers where curriculum
guides are arranged by a simple notation system while the
children's literature collection uses the Dewey Decimal Classification system. Reference books, textbooks, and supplementary instructional materials, both print and nonprint, are
usually cataloged in technical service areas. This occurs
even where the Dewey system is used for this material while
the remainder of the library's collection is classified by the
Library of Congress system. Even when processed in the
center, books and media should be classified by the DDC or
LC systems since good cataloging copy is available using
these classification systems. Library of Congress cards can
be ordered or commercial services offer cards for much of
this material.

There are real problems in deciding on a subject heading list. The Library of Congress, Sears, and Education In-

dex are all used. The Thesaurus of ERIC Descriptors is highly recommended by curriculum librarians. (It is available from Oryx Press, 2214 North Central at Encanto, Phoenix, Arizona 85004.) Rapid changes in education and adoption of popular terms make it common in most catalogs to add subject headings or at least referral cards for such terms as "mainstreaming" or "learning centers" before LC has chosen to use these terms. Many curriculum centers were using "mainstreaming" before LC chose to use "mainstreaming in education" as the correct term, and material on learning centers was put under that term when the LC heading still used was "open plan schools" and "individualized instruction."

When Cutter numbers are added to a Dewey or special classification number, they usually represent the publisher on textbooks and their accompanying manuals and on publishers' series of enrichment reading materials. This is done because the material is so often the product of a committee or of several authors, no one of whom plays a significant role. Nonbook media often are the product of the producing company rather than of an individual. Single monographs and children's literature use the Cutter number for the author. On courses of study or curriculum guides, the Cutter number may represent the issuing agency, a school or a bureau of the department of education.

Ellis said, "It is generally felt that the card catalog can render more service if all materials are represented in one index," but she saw pamphlets, book jackets and magazines as exceptions to this rule. She also felt that all cards should be interfiled, rather than making a separate catalog for different forms of materials.[11] Actually many other separate collections may exist for nonprint or microform materials, tests, maps, curriculum guides, or textbooks, and different classification systems and different levels of cataloging and classification may be used for one or more of these. Brief systems may need to be used for materials which have a short life, and indexing may be so brief and incomplete that it does not make sense to add it to the center's general catalog. If material is already indexed by the publisher (e.g., curriculum guides on microfiche), it may be more sensible to add other guides to that index than to catalog them in the more traditional way. Brief computerized indexes or KWIC systems may be less expensive than full cataloging for ephemeral items. Sometimes states revise each subject area only once in five or six years and mate-

rials added to a collection for such a period of time should
be fully cataloged.

Wide variations occur in the classification of audiovisual materials. Sometimes they are arranged only chrono-
logically by accession numbers or in groups by form with a
form prefix letter. These systems require a subject catalog
and are not easy to browse. More often a Dewey system is
used without any subdivision by form but with a form notation as part of the call number. Color coding by form,
once a popular practice, is not recommended. This system
has broken down as a result of the large number of forms
available, the wider use of multi-media kits and because
color coding required local processing rather than the use
of national systems or cards from commercial vendors.
Multimedia materials need the addition of age level and
grade and, if the clientele demands it, the producer and the
artists appearing as performers.

The description for audiovisual materials uses brief
symbols to indicate the elements of interest to the users.
These abbreviations include:

b&w	black and white
ea	each
fps	frames per second
"	inches, disc diameter
ips	inches per second
min	minutes
mm	millimeter
mono	monaural
rpm	revolutions per minute
s	sides
sd	sound
si	silent
stereo	stereophonic

These descriptive abbreviations can be confusing, and a more
complete and better differentiated notation is suggested by the
AECT Standards for Cataloging. [12]

Some common principles which are applied in most
situations are:

1. If a title has two forms, e.g., filmstrip and
cassette, which are to be filed separately,
each item should bear a notation to refer the

user to the other item[13]

2. Color coding of cards for different forms of material is inefficient and expensive and its use is practical only in very small collections which do not have many types of media

3. Whenever possible the media item as well as the box should bear the call number; this requires writing on the tape or film leader with a flow-tip pen

4. Commercial boxes, labels, tags, and stickers designed for media can be used effectively.

A new book by Nancy B. Olson, Cataloging Audiovisual Materials: A Manual Based on AACR2, (Mankato, Minnesota: Minnesota Scholarly Press, 1980) may help in the cataloging process.

Ellis recommended that award-winning books be shelved separately in the reference or reserve section, either by author or by year.[14] By year is probably only appropriate if the collection is a duplicate one. Retrieval will be easier if full cataloging is used so that author or illustrator can be an entry point.

Courses of study need entries for subject, broken down by grade level, producer, and title. Often several subjects are involved; for example an item might fall both under reading and bilingual education. Curriculum guides or units can be handled in the same way and interfiled since courses of study often include curriculum guides. Grade level is often considered more important than subject, due to the interdisciplinary nature of some curriculum guides, and if curriculum guides are kept as a separate collection, grade level would be appropriate for the primary arrangement. However, where they are combined with courses of study, a subject arrangement with grade level as a sub-arrangement makes more sense. Some centers arrange curriculum guides by subject in alphabetical order, subdivided by state of origin, without maintaining any catalog. It is also not uncommon to find curriculum guides and courses of study for the home state as a separate arrangement, with all other materials of this type grouped together. MacVean's analysis of cataloging needs includes having analytics for units which appear in courses of study.[15] While it is true that guides and units are somewhat lost within a course of study, the cost of analyzing such material would seem to be almost an impossibility for most curriculum centers.

Ellis suggested that maps be arranged by countries.[16] If the collection is substantial, they should be classified and cataloged and will then fall in this order, with a subject subarrangement.

Tests need to be maintained as a separate collection because of special security considerations, and they probably need a locked file with an open index. Tests may be arranged by author or producing body, or by type--such as intelligence, aptitude, or achievement. A test classification scheme was developed by Walter W. Durost and Margaret E. Allen at Boston University.

General pamphlet files, which might include bulletin board materials and book jackets, can be filed by subject. Vertical files may need to be broken down into two categories: education and general. Subject headings for vertical files or picture files should be taken from a standard list such as the Vertical File Index or Education Index, or one of the standard picture file listings. New areas in education seem to arise and become popular long before these sources adopt a new subject heading, so it is necessary to add to the subject heading list for new items. Unfortunately, this often means a change when the new form is officially adopted.

There are also some general assumptions about how textbooks should be handled. It is generally accepted that they should be arranged by subject, subdivided by publisher and grade level. For example, using the Dewey classification a call number might be:

T501
G434c
Gr. 4

The T stands for textbook, followed by a Dewey subject number. The G434 is a Cutter number for the publisher, and the small c indicates author, editor or title as appropriate. The grade level is also indicated. If symbols are added for teacher's edition, manual, or workbook, these should appear at the end of a common call number in order to place the textbook with its accompanying supplementary items. The textbook can have full cataloging, like other materials, but recognition should always be given to the addition of a form designation, the need for grade level and the identification of the producer--often the publisher rather than an author or editor.

Many curriculum materials centers have a file of pictures. This may include posters, diagrams, charts, graphs, flip charts, and flannel boards. These items are combined and used in preparing bulletin boards, signs, flannel boards, dioramas, mobiles, multimedia programs, and for direct instruction. The uses in a classroom are well described in The Picture File by Donna Hill. [17] Other relevant books are Teaching Displays by Mona Garvey (Hamden, Conn.: Linnet Books, 1972) and The Picture Collection Subject Headings by William Dane (Hamden, Conn.: The Shoe String Press, 1968). In the materials production center, pictures are often used in the preparation of slides or filmstrips or as backgrounds or a collage.

In some curriculum centers the problem of obtaining copyright permission for duplicating pictures is seen as the responsibility of the user who borrows a picture. Users are not queried to see if they plan to duplicate the picture in another media form--as part of a slide, microfiche or video program, for example. Section 107 of the copyright law would seem to allow the reproduction of a picture for one classroom use under certain conditions, but it may be appropriate to remind future teachers of possible copyright restrictions and to direct them to materials available on copyright. Commercial clip books can be used for pictures, and copyright problems do not arise in this case.

In storing and organizing a picture file, transparencies are sometimes included and interfiled. This may be appropriate for single transparencies, but commercial sets on a single subject should probably be cataloged as a set and kept with other print and-or nonprint materials.

Flandro found one respondent who indicated that they had a picture file of schools, classrooms, and playgrounds classified by subjects such as "reading activities" or "science experiences." [18]

One of the subject headings listed in the books mentioned previously can form the organization for a picture file. A card file or computerized index will define the scope of each subject heading, with "search under" and "search also under" cards to refer the user to the correct subject. Dry-mounted and laminated pictures can have labels attached which indicate an accession number, the subject, and source. By using hanging file folders, the pictures stored in a vertical file can be protected somewhat against damage. Pictures are usually circulated in a sturdy envelope with cardboard added to prevent folding or bending. A collection of over-size pictures is usually stored in flat map cases, and the location is indicated by adding to the file a referral card on the subject covered.

Special Classification Systems

While the Library of Congress and Dewey Decimal systems are the most popular classification schemes, many others are used and probably no one scheme is actually used in a majority of curriculum materials collections. Classifi-cation is usually kept as simple as possible; for example, Dewey is only used to three digits, reflecting the need to group by broad subject fields. Special notations include such things as the use of T for textbook and TM or M for a teachers' manual. The collection is sometimes divided to-tally by elementary and secondary grades, or it may be in-tegrated by subject and then subdivided by level. One fairly representative system uses a call number such as this:

E Sci	E = elementary, Sci = science
SS	S = publisher (Scott-Foresman), S = title
4	4 = grade level

Another system uses a letter code for the form first and spells out the grade level in the notation:

L	L = textbook
E Sci	
SS	
gr. 4	

The coding system at the Pueblo School in Scottsdale, Arizona, as described in Pergeau, also tries to meet specific teaching needs in its notation:

SC3 - P7 *a*

This indicates a science unit for third grade, specifically for physical science. The 7 indicates the concept of space and the a refers to the skill of observing. The asterisk is used to indicate that more than just the skill shown is in-volved.[19] The fourth element (space, in the example above) might be one of many elements when used in social studies material; twenty-nine elements are listed. Mathematics breaks down even further, into great detail in some areas:

MA3 - S4 b

Here MA = mathematics, 3 = grade 3, S = sets, 4 = set
identification, and b = subset. [20]

A common problem for users of curriculum collections is that too many separate files are maintained. While
this may be appropriate for centers which do not have the
support of a technical services unit, in the academic library
situation the files may have fewer divisions, and more material can be cataloged for the main collection. Some materials, because of their content or physical form, will still
be kept separate. These may include the test file, the picture file, a file of publishers' catalogs and brochures, unpublished teaching aids such as units of work, lesson plans
prepared by students, and a general pamphlet file, which
often includes some of the other items. Maps and charts
which are large in size and fragile in nature may have to
be filed in large flat drawers of map cabinets. Microfiche
have become more common in recent years and contribute
to the proliferation of separate files and collections.

There is some argument about whether or not cards
should be put in the card catalog for all of these items.
Items which are not adequately described and are short-lived
may be better indexed in a separate card file adjacent to the
material--as with picture files--or by a simple computerized
list. The main card catalog for the center, however, may
need cross-reference cards which lead the patron from the
subject area in the catalog to other materials on the same
subject which appear in special files. A card such as the
following might be inserted in the catalog:

> SUBJECT
>
> For further information on this
> subject, see the following files:
>
>   TEST FILE
>   PAMPHLET FILE
>   PICTURE FILE

If the center has access to a simple sorting program at the
computer service center, it may be appropriate to list the
subjects on a printout which can either be posted near the

file or placed in the front of the first drawer. Such a printout may be easier to maintain than a card file and can easily
be updated and re-formated by the computer for production
of revised lists. A notation system could be used on each
item which in the index would be purely a location aid.

If curriculum guides and courses of study are represented in the main catalog, Cox suggested that a card be
produced for each entry under the producing location.[21] This
would enable users to find all of the publications from particular school systems where they had been assigned for student teaching, or to find material from a school whose guides
and courses of study have a reputation for quality. Labeling
of curriculum guides is often a problem since the covers are
easily torn off. A call number on an inside page is necessary. Where to place the label on the cover depends on
whether the material is to be stored in files or in pamphlet
boxes on a shelf.

Cox's manual recommends that textbooks be classified
by subject, subdivided by publisher, using the Dewey Decimal
Classification system. For example:

> T300 Social Sciences
> T400 Language Arts
> T500 Science
> T600 Useful Arts
> T700 Fine Arts[22]

Since the Dewey system allows for expansion to represent
the curriculum breakdown, expansion or contraction depending
upon the size of the collection is easily facilitated. The decimal numbers can be used to arrange supplementary books and
media following the textbook on the same subject.[23] Cox
stated the purposes of the system to be:

> 1) Through this system of cataloging, all books in
>   the same subject area will be located together
>   on the shelves. Along with each text will be
>   found the teacher's manual, tests and workbooks
>   which directly supplement the text.
> 2) The publisher's series will be kept together.
>   Keeping publishers' series together is important
>   since each series develops a complete program
>   within an area of the school curriculum. [24]

Under Cox's system the call number would then be:

"T511
W893g

This number is assigned to World Book Company's GROWTH IN ARITHMETIC SERIES. "[25] Grade level could be added.

While textbooks seldom have an author as the single responsible person, a senior editor's name could be used in the Cutter number. The series title is always more important than the individual title, although the latter can be used for the purpose of identifying the individual item.

Several curriculum centers have a note indicating which parts of a series the library possesses. This can be more complicated with language arts series, since so many items in the series should be listed in the order in which they will be used.[26]

Subject headings have to represent the purpose of the material. That is, a book may be about dogs or cats but its subject heading would be "Readers, Basal."

As part of her dissertation, Ellis prepared a manual for processing curriculum materials titled A Manual of Procedures for Processing of Book and Non-Book Materials in Curriculum Centers. She recommended using the number subject scheme from Textbooks in Print as the subject classification. This scheme groups the detailed subjects together under a broad subject heading which corresponds to the school curriculum:

28   Composition, Creative Writing
29   English
30   Handwriting
31   Journalism
32   Language
33   Library Guidance
34   Literature
34. 1 Classics
34. 2 Poetry, Poets
34. 3 Stories
34. 4 Authors
35. 5 Heroes

Reading would be under "Readers, Basal" as follows:

    36   Reading Readiness
    37   Programmed Reading Materials
    38   Reading Skills, Remedial, Phonics
    39   Speech
    40   Spelling[27]

Because the system is expansible, it can be modified with geographic or historical period breakdowns.

Ellis recommended a mnemonic abbreviation for the form of material, e.g., FS for filmstrip, MK for media kit. Thus a media kit on heroes would have the call number:

    MK   form
    34.5 subject
    24   accession number

with the grade level appearing in the upper right hand corner of the card rather than as part of the call number.

One curriculum materials center uses a mnemonic system of classification for its curriculum guides and courses of study. While at first this may seem somewhat complicated and unfamiliar to the user, once the system is understood, it becomes easy to use and self-explanatory. The call number would look like this:

    CS   CS = Course of study
    Ma/E   MA = Mathematics, E = Elementary
    6   6 = grade level
    IL/Chi   Chi = Chicago Public Schools

Categories of materials sometimes have subclassification letters. For example: RF:Z is a reference bibliography. Subjects can be handled either as Dewey numbers or mnemonic letters, e.g., 324.4 or SOC SCI.

While not all curriculum materials centers do it, there does seem to be real value in including in a notation the information that the item is a state-adopted title. This can be done by a designation preceding the call number, as is done at the San Jose State University center. Their call number, using Dewey and a Cutter number for title appears as:

    State text
    372.4
    R287

Since both student teachers and community users desire this information, it is worth the addition. The main problem, of course, is the removal of the information when the item has been superseded as a state-adopted text, but is nevertheless kept for its own value. The call number also becomes more complicated when the item also includes type of material:

    State text
    535
    B595h
    K-gr. 6
    filmstrip set

The adoption designation is not really a part of the call number and is not used in shelving the book.

Probably the most popular system for organizing curriculum collections is the one devised for the Educational Materials Laboratory at the Office of Education, International Studies and Services, revised in 1962 and 1967 by Lois Belfield Watt. The system permits a subclassification under the 370 class of the Dewey Decimal Classification or can be used with just an initial letter/subject classification in collections limited only to curriculum materials. [28]

The first four letters of the scheme are used for supplementary material (A for reference books, C for children's literature), while the letters E through Z are assigned to textbooks by curriculum subjects (J for science, M for music, N for art). [29] Decimal numbers are used to break down subjects into specific areas. A small e or s is used to indicate elementary or secondary level. Thus Ee. 2 would be English, elementary, plus .2 to represent reading. A further breakdown is possible by adding to the decimal number. Thus Ee. 21 would be English, elementary, phonics as a subset of reading. [30]

The notation then identifies the specific item by a Cutter number, using either a letter or a letter and number for the publisher's name and grade level, and a small letter for title. A date is added to distinguish editions. [31] Thus a call number might be:

    Ms. 3
    S10i
    1980

for a book on music appreciation for tenth grade published

by Smith Publishers and titled <u>Introduction to Music Appreciation</u>. In this example M = music, s = secondary, .3 = music appreciation, S = Smith Publishers, 10 = grade ten, and i = title. Classifications can also be combined. "Such a book as <u>Algebra for Electronics</u> could be classed Ts. 44:Ks3 and shelved following all books dealing only with electronics. "[32]

This classification scheme brings the books into the most useful arrangement for browsing an area of the shelves. The author describes its arrangement:

> The textbooks classified according to this scheme are arranged on the shelves of the Laboratory, <u>first</u>, according to the curriculum area in which they are used (English, social studies, science, etc.); <u>second</u>, according to whether they are elementary or secondary school books; <u>third</u>, according to the course they are prepared for (history, geography, civics, etc.).
> Within each course the books are arranged, <u>first</u>, according to the alphabetical order of their publishers' names; <u>second</u>, by grade level, and <u>third</u> (and only if necessary to distinguish separate titles), by author. [33]

A form notation (film, filmstrip) can either precede the call number or follow it depending on whether the collection is to be kept separate by form or integrated into each subject area regardless of form. A curriculum center using the system also adds to the call number a notation indicating state adoption, if appropriate. A teacher's edition, manual or workbook which accompanies the textbook may be given the same call number as the textbook but a TE, M or W is added below the call number so that these supplements to the textbook are shelved immediately after it.

This Office of Education <u>Textbook Classification Scheme</u> has appeared in a fifth revision; this latest version was prepared by Marietta L. Harper, a consultant at the Educational Materials Review Center. Available as an ERIC document, the new system was prepared to take into account "the advent of new curriculum materials for Math, Science, Special Education, Career Education, Foreign Language and Social Studies. "[34] Arrangement on the shelf in the Educational Materials Review Center does not separate elementary and secondary books, although the system suggests that the e (elementary) and s (secondary) could be continued from former editions, and it permits the use of j (junior high) or m (middle school). The new schedules have added more foreign languages such as Vietnamese, Yoruba, and Swahili, and Mathematics has added integrated mathematics, calculus, and metric system. Classes are also included for bilingual education and adult education materials.

In 1971, Robert E. Jones proposed a system based on subject areas appearing in the National Study of Secondary School Evaluation, Evaluative Criteria (Washington, D.C.: National Study of Secondary School Evaluation, 1960). Jones separated textbooks, manuals, and curriculum guides into three separate collections. Curriculum guides included courses of study, syllabi, and resource units. Both the textbook and curriculum guide collections were divided first by level--each with its own color designation for early childhood, elementary, middle school, or junior high, high school, and junior college. Jones wrote:

> The scheme for arranging and/or organizing the curriculum guide collection provides a shelf arrangement and a shelf list organized in the following hierarchy: (a) grade level, (b) subject, (c) author, and (d) title. That for the textbooks provides a shelf arrangement and a shelf list organized according to (a) grade level, (b) subject, (c) publisher, and (d) title, while the manuals are organized according to (a) topic, (b) author, and (c) title. [35]

The call number for a manual could thus be:

M
S6.6
D4

Here the M stands for a manual, the LC "Author Number" stands for the subject--social work, and the D4 represents the source or publisher, also expressed with an LC "Author Number." If an author were involved, a lower case letter representing his/her name could be added to the S6.6 subject designation. The first sort would, of course, have been by the color designator for grade level. [36]

This relatively simple system, using the Anglo-American rules for the descriptive cataloging and available

from ERIC, is a useful system for a small collection and
could be easily implemented and converted to AACR2 rules
by catalogers familiar with the Library of Congress system
of classification and cataloging.

An adaptation of the Library of Congress classification system for use with non-fiction children's books has
been developed by the staff of the Inglewood Public Library,
Inglewood, California. It has been continually revised and
updated and includes other media as well as books. The
system uses the general classification--one or two letters
with number classes added where a more detailed breakdown
is required. This manual, which is made more useful by a
subject index, makes it possible to use the LC system while
maintaining the advantage of grouping materials in the broad
subject classes appropriate for children's materials. [37]

Classification for Individual Needs

With the increasing availability of computer services
able to bring together several elements in various combinations as needed, the classification of curriculum materials
is beginning to be seen as a problem of matching the material to the needs of the individual child rather than a system
for arranging materials on a shelf.

A dissertation by Donald Lee Pack described several
of these systems and studied the Annehurst Curriculum
Classification System in detail. Some of the systems designed for retrieval of suitable material for the individual
and used for curriculum materials are:

1. Prescriptive Materials Retrieval System
2. Educational Patterns, Inc. (E. P. I.)
3. Far West Laboratory Library Classification
   System
4. Great Lakes Regional Special Education Instructional Materials Center
5. Annehurst Curriculum Classification System. [38]

The Prescriptive Materials Retrieval System is designed to match instructional material to specific learning
problems. It can be used either manually or on the computer. It has over 400 descriptors in eight major categories
and uses a six-step approach to match the material to the
student. More complete information on the system is avail-

able in Prescriptive Materials Retrieval System prepared by
B. L. Winch and Associates (Torrence, California: B. L.
Winch and Associates, 1973), and in Educational Descriptor
Dictionary for the Prescriptive Materials Retrieval System by
Carlson Van Etten and Gary Adamson (Lenexa, Kansas:
Select-Ed, Inc., 1973).[39]

The Educational Patterns, Inc. system, which is also
designed for the individual student's needs, uses a system of
sorting cards. It classifies material by skill, level, modali-
ties, interest, format, and interaction. It uses an alphabetical designator for each of 22 skills. Further information is
available in The E. P. I. Retrieval System: Guide (Rego Park,
New York: Educational Patterns Incorporated, 1974).[40]

In 1972 Marda Woodbury described the system used at
the Far West Laboratory for Educational Research and Development at Berkeley, California. She felt that LC and DDC
were not adequate as classification systems for education materials because their approach to education was historical and
did not reflect modern theory or practice. She also felt that
the ERIC system was too unsystematic.

The system she recommended used the 26 letters to
break down education into areas, with the more general aspects coming in the first few letters:

    A = Reference
    B = Research
    C = Child
    H = Teachers and Teaching
    Z = Evaluation[41]

Each category can be subdivided by a mnemonic designation:

    AM = Maps
    AP = Publishers' catalogs
    AR = Annual reports
    CD = Disadvantaged children
    CP = The child as pupil
    ZA = Accountability

Color codes are also used:

    Red = Pamphlets
    Brown = Curriculum[42]

The system is interesting because it organizes materials into
sensible education relationships (for example, I = Methods of
Instruction) and breaks down into items such as:

IA = Assignments
ID = Discussion
IP = Programmed instruction
IT = Team Teaching
TU = Tutoring[43]

All of the categories listed are not necessarily related to curriculum materials. Many are for professional
education literature and are more useful for education research, the main emphasis at Berkeley. The system's use-
fulness however, is apparent for curriculum guides, reports,
educational research reports, and an educational pamphlet
file.

Another system which classifies materials to match
the characteristics of the learner was developed at the
Great Lakes Region Special Education Instructional Materials
Center. Designed for children with hearing handicaps, the
system involves a careful diagnosis of the learner's academic
needs and matches the material to such elements as mental
and chronological age, performance grade level, social development, emotional development, and cognitive development.
This permits materials to be classified to match the child
whose development is in stage one for some variables but in
stage two or three for others. Each stage and variable is
carefully defined so that the level of the child's need can be
determined.

In this system, all materials are examined for intent
of use by the child, on one of three levels: minimal for
enjoyment, instructional for learning, and competency for
mastery of the concepts. Each item of instructional material
has a descriptive statement relating its content to the stage
of development of children.[44]

The Annehurst System is best described by Frymier
in Annehurst Curriculum Classification System: A Practical
Way to Individualize Instruction. This system, used at the
Annehurst Elementary School in Westerville, Ohio, was developed by that school's staff and five members of the Faculty
of Curriculum and Foundations at the Ohio State University,
and was designed to "facilitate the assigning of curriculum
materials to students on the basis of individual differences."[45]

This system teaches the assessment of individual learners' characteristics as they relate to school work and classifies materials in similar terms. Using these characteristics, the system organizes the material for later retrieval. [46] Frymier calls the system a "linking mechanism" to "maximize learning." [47] It is suggested that the system is best used by a group of teachers sharing a pool of curriculum materials. From this collection of materials, teachers can set up learning centers, vary time expectations to meet students' learning rates and use a more individual teaching methodology. [48] The system is expansible to permit new disciplines or topics and does not require new editions to keep it up to date.

The material to be analyzed under the Annehurst system is not the large set or complete textbook but rather the item with a single concept, such as pamphlets, workbooks, filmstrips, worksheets, and other single-page items. [49] The system permits the bringing together of many small, single items to create a package of materials needed to teach a concept or groups of concepts. It gives the teacher the responsibility of choosing the material, on the assumption that only the teacher knows both the student and the subject matter and can bring the two together for maximum effect. It is assumed under this system that all materials are included, for example, those for a large range of age groups and those presenting all kinds of views (those of the Flat Earth Society as well as those who believe the earth is a sphere), and not necessarily assigned to any one subject. [50]

Classification by learning needs uses these curriculum characteristics; experience, intelligence, motivation, emotion, personality, creativity, social, verbal expression, auditory perception, visual perception, and motor perception. [51] The subject breakdown employs a thesaurus which can include 1000 topics per discipline, dividing one discipline into ten major subjects, 1000 subject divisions, and then 1000 topics. [52]

The notation comes from the thesaurus. For example, the index to the thesaurus shows: Aging, Physiology as #7132.

7 = Biological Science
1 = Human body
3 = Physiology
2 = Aging

The work sheet for the materials classification shows:

media   3 = transparency
age group   b = 9-12

Other characteristics are defined as appropriate or not appropriate, as high or low. [53]

      Obviously the system is particularly useful with computer searching. The application of computer technology to the organization of curriculum materials seems to be in just its embryo stage. Libraries are addressing the increased capability for cataloging materials provided by OCLC, MARC format and AACR2 descriptions and as Boolean subject searching is used in automated circulation systems. An appropriate coordination of the library's programs in this area with the systems developed by professional educators might well bring about a totally different way of handling the organization of curriculum materials. The ease of altering computerized records is especially important where a collection has a limited life. The matching of the several variables of curriculum materials in combinations for individual needs can clearly be achieved more effectively by a computerized system. Librarians concerned about curriculum materials need to bring their expertise in machine-readable bibliographic records to the curriculum materials problem.

Conclusion

      The practices which have resulted in so many ways of organizing instructional materials in curriculum materials centers have not followed the pattern of the cataloging process in academic libraries nationally. Whereas the trend in academic libraries has been towards national standards and integrated systems using computer technology, the trend in handling curriculum materials is still toward diversity and, in many cases, experimentation. Experimentation which results in analysis of the content of materials should continue, but classification and cataloging systems designed for the organization of materials on a shelf or in a file would benefit from the efficiencies that result from national standards and cooperative systems.

NOTES

[1]Donald S. MacVean, "A Study of Curriculum Laboratories in

Midwestern Teacher Training Institutions" (Doctoral Dissertation, University of Michigan, 1958), p. 90.

[2] Carl Cox, The Curriculum Laboratory: An Organizational Manual (Nashville, Tennessee: George Peabody College for Teachers, Library Science Graduate School, 1961), p. 90.

[3] Helen Mae Arnett, "Accessibility of Instructional Materials with Implications for the Organization of Curriculum Laboratories" (Doctoral Dissertation, Western Reserve University, 1965), p. 106.

[4] Harlan R. Johnson, "The Curriculum Materials Center: A Study of Policies and Practices" (Doctoral Dissertation, Northern Arizona University, 1973), p. 33.

[5] Cora Paul Bomar, M. Ann Heidbreder, and Carol A. Nemeyer, Guide to the Development of Educational Media Selection Centers (Chicago: American Library Association, 1976), p. 51.

[6] MacVean, "A Study of Curriculum Laboratories, " p. ii.

[7] Johnson, "The Curriculum Materials Center," p. 16.

[8] Ibid., p. 43.

[9] MacVean, "A Study of Curriculum Laboratories, " p. 88.

[10] Janice Gallinger, "Educational Media Selection Centers and Academic Libraries." Paper presented at the Annual Meeting of the American Library Association (ED 095 838) (New York, July, 1974), p. 6.

[11] Eleanor V. Ellis, The Role of the Curriculum Laboratory in the Preparation of Quality Teachers (Tallahassee, Fl.: Florida A&M Foundation, Inc., 1969), p. 54.

[12] Alma Tillin and William J. Quinly, Standards for Cataloging Nonprint Materials, 4th ed. (Washington, D.C.: Association for Educational Communications and Technology, 1976), p. 222.

[13] Ibid., p. 114.

[14] Ellis, The Role of the Curriculum Laboratory, p. 52.

148 / Managing Curriculum Materials

[15] MacVean, "A Study of Curriculum Laboratories," p. 13.

[16] Ellis, The Role of the Curriculum Laboratory, p. 52.

[17] Donna Hill, The Picture File: A Manual and Curriculum Related Subject Heading List (Hamden, Conn.: Shoestring Press, 1975), pp. 49-70.

[18] Royce P. Flandro, "Curriculum Laboratories in Colleges of Teacher Education" (Doctoral Dissertation, Indiana University, 1957), p. 169.

[19] Scottsdale, Arizona Public Schools, Keeping Order: Coding-Materials, Audio Visual Aids, and Microfiche. Staff Utilization for Continuous Progress Education Project, E. S. E. A. Title III (ED 088 426), Beverly Pergeau, coordinator (Scottsdale, Ariz.: Scottsdale Public Schools, 1973), p. 3.

[20] Ibid., p. 6-20.

[21] Cox, The Curriculum Laboratory, p. 37.

[22] Ibid., pp. 46-47.

[23] Ibid., pp. 47-48.

[24] Ibid., p. 49.

[25] Ibid., p. 51.

[26] Ibid., p. 58.

[27] Ellis, The Role of the Curriculum Laboratory, pp. 4-5.

[28] Lois Belfield Watt, A Classification Scheme for Elementary and Secondary School Textbooks in Educational Materials Centers, Educational Materials Laboratory Report IV, no. 1 (Washington, D. C.: Government Printing Office, 1962), p. 3.

[29] Ibid., p. 7.

[30] Ibid., p. 13.

[31] Ibid., p. 4.

[32] Ibid., p. 5.

[33] Ibid., p. 4.

[34] Lois Belfield Watt, Textbook Classification Scheme: For Use with Elementary and Secondary Curriculum Materials in Instructional Materials Centers, revised by Marietta L. Harper (ED 181 914) (Washington, D.C.: U.S. Department of Education, Educational Materials Review Center, 1979), p. 1.

[35] Robert E. Jones, "A Proposed Classification Schedule for a Curriculum Materials Collection" (ED 070 464) (Master's Thesis, Central Washington State College, 1971), p. 13.

[36] Ibid., p. 72.

[37] John W. Perkins, "An Adapted Library of Congress Classification for Children's Materials," Library Resources and Technical Services 22 (Spring, 1978): 175-177.

[38] Donald Lee Pack, "A Study of the Interclassifier Reliability in Relation to the Annehurst Curriculum Classification System" (Doctoral Dissertation, Drake University, 1978), pp. 21-27.

[39] Ibid., pp. 21-23.

[40] Ibid., p. 23.

[41] Marda Woodbury, Rationale and Schedule for a Classification System for Education and Education Related Materials (ED 070 458) (Berkeley, California: Far West Laboratory for Educational Research and Development, 1972), p. 3.

[42] Ibid., p. 4.

[43] Ibid., p. 27.

[44] Nancy A. Carlson, Cynthia A. Lafkas, and S. Joseph Levine, Bridging the Gap Between Materials and Learners: Maximizing Auditory Instruction, (ED 102 753) (Consortium on Auditory Learning Materials for the Handicapped, 1974), pp. 3-13.

[45] Pack, "A Study of the Interclassifier Reliability," p. 2.

[46] Jack R. Frymier, <u>The Annehurst Curriculum Classification System: A Practical Way to Individualize Instruction</u> (West Lafayette, Indiana: Kappa Delta Pi, 1977), p. 1.

[47] Ibid., p. 4.

[48] Ibid., p. 7.

[49] Ibid., p. 32.

[50] Ibid., p. 41.

[51] Ibid., pp. 166-169.

[52] Ibid., p. 173.

[53] Ibid., p. 277.

CHAPTER 8

MANAGING THE SERVICES OF THE
CURRICULUM MATERIALS CENTER

Dedicating Personnel to the Service Component

In the study he did back in 1946, Francis Drag said that: "Resources and facilities alone no more constitute a curriculum laboratory than does a staff of curriculum leaders without the necessary facilities and resources."[1] To blend the elements of the curriculum materials center into a functional unit a professional staff dedicated to the provision of service is essential. A successful curriculum materials center supplies the service activities which make its collection and facilities useful to the clientele.

Donald S. MacVean, a frequent writer on the subject of curriculum collections, found that the uses of curriculum materials centers, in order of frequency, were: "(1) to examine materials to be familiar with them, (2) to select materials for classroom use, (3) to locate material to build units, (4) to prepare lesson plans."[2] To meet this demand and to encourage growth in the quantity and expansion of types of service, a wide variety of service activities are necessary. These services need both to meet existing demand and to create new demands through programs of orientation, instruction, and public relations. The services of the center should include such tasks as:

1. Maintaining the collection in good order for retrieval
2. Maintaining a catalog or other aids for retrieving materials in the collection
3. Assisting students in identifying materials useful to them in preparing units, lesson plans, and other teaching programs
4. Assisting patrons in identifying materials to teach selection and evaluation

151

5. Teaching students the broad nature of materials in the collection which can be useful to them
6. Delivering and otherwise encouraging use of the media in classes and other group meetings
7. Advising students about manuals and how-to-do-it books useful in their course work for materials production or learning center construction
8. Giving students instruction and practice in operating equipment
9. Implementing policies in a fair and efficient manner
10. Keeping good records on orders, acquisitions, supplies, and circulating items
11. Maintaining facilities and equipment that contribute to the primary functions of the center
12. Giving class tours and group tours
13. Giving class lectures
14. Compiling bibliographies and guides to the media
15. Circulating materials
16. Collecting reviews and evaluations
17. Conducting research to improve services
18. Coordinating services with other campus and community agencies which offer similar functions or supplementary functions
19. Cooperating with other curriculum materials centers and curriculum collections.

Dedicated personnel are necessary if all of these functions are to be carried on. Substantial cataloging activity in the curriculum materials center is frequently a poor use of expensive personnel. If the curriculum center staff needs to take on some other shared activity, rotating them with other reference librarians is more beneficial to the patron who thus encounters people who know both collections and can make good referrals to materials in the other area. Releasing personnel from technical processing chores, some of which are routine and clerical in nature, permits the center's staff to spend their time on better public relations or to be more involved in classroom lectures and student contact.

Maintaining the Collection

Because the emphasis in curriculum materials centers

has become the provision of the collection, maintaining it in the most effective way to assist retrieval by users is a major service function. Maintenance includes arrangement of the different types of materials within the center, preserving the materials and equipment, and maintaining a continual search for the best way to make the collection useful to the clientele of the center. Regardless of the classification system used, many decisions have to be made on the arrangement of special types of materials, based on: 1) the physical form of some materials, 2) their fragile nature, 3) their nature as a special collection, and 4) their pattern of use.

The organization of these special types of materials requires careful analysis if the materials are to be easy to find and retrieve. The central philosophy should be the same as that for any library--that all materials should be arranged by some standard classification system in a single collection. Just as this philosophy is violated in most library situations, so it is with great frequency when arranging curriculum materials. The reasons for variations and separate arrangements may be: 1) non-standard form, 2) the need to have certain materials near personnel (e.g., reference books), 3) uncataloged material (e.g., ephemeral in nature such as certain pamphlets), 4) the need for security (e.g., standardized tests), and 5) the pattern of use (e.g., periodicals).

Some divisions of the collection will probably occur in all curriculum materials centers, but no two centers seem to make the same decisions on these arrangements. Materials for grades 7-12 may be separated from those for kindergarten through grade 6. These are often totally separate collections, even though having a grade breakdown under the general subject is more efficient because of the obvious overlaps from grade to grade. HiLo materials (high interest-low reading level) are often separated from other materials for the user's convenience, since teachers may be searching only for this type of material. Reference books, picture books, foreign language materials, or materials forming a "special collection" may also be shelved separately. The size of easy readers and picture books may make separation desirable when shelving is tight and oversize materials cannot be accommodated in the general collection. Audiovisual media are often kept separate because of the variety of forms and the difficulty of shelving very large kits, oversize chart sets, and other large forms.

There are arguments about the separation of textbooks

and their accompanying materials from supplementary fiction
and nonfiction.   If textbooks are kept as a separate collection, they can be arranged in publishers' series order.   Arguments for this are that faculty usually refer students to
such material by the publisher's name and series.   This arrangement permits a student to survey the whole series, relating the texts for one grade with those for the preceding
and subsequent grades.   Another less compelling argument
is that a publisher's representative is more generous in
presenting free textbooks if the whole product of his company
is kept isolated.   Against these advantages must be weighed
the desirability of a user's finding all materials on one subject and grade level in the same place.   The ability to
browse a single area which contains all (or nearly all) of
the needed materials is especially useful to students and beginning teachers.   There is fairly general agreement that
each textbook must be accompanied by its supplementary
teacher's edition, manual and workbooks.   Smith and Gardner
recommended that the books, workbooks, and manuals should
be shelved together[3] and Arnett found, in visits to fourteen
NCATE colleges, that the workbooks needed to be with the
textbooks or they would not be used as much.   Arnett also
found that courses of study or curriculum guides were not
extensively used if they were not cataloged and thus a part
of the general arrangement. [4]

It is, however, a common practice to keep curriculum
guides (and courses of study) as a separate collection.   This
may be because of their fragile physical form, with paper
covers and spiral backs.   Curriculum guides and courses of
study, if separated, can be kept in vertical files or in pamphlet files on a shelf.   A very general breakdown can be
used if they are not cataloged.   Often recommended is a
mnemonic system using a notation such as BUS for business,
ED for education, followed by grade level and then arrangement by the producing body, such as a school system or a
state department.   Where microfiche are used for the collection, the hard copy collection may be small and, for convenience, shelved adjacent to the microfiche collection, its
titles being added to one of the microfiche indexes.   If the
microfiche set of curriculum guides is large, it may be
stored in cabinets with other large collections such as the
ERIC collection.   If the curriculum center has only a small
amount of microfiche, it might be more appropriate to shelve
it together with hard copy materials.   For example, back
runs of serials might be stored in a looseleaf notebook type
of holder along with recent paper issues.

Other materials which may be separated are large kits, transparencies, disc recordings, or large realia items such as globes. Most media forms can be boxed, marked, and shelved like books and do not need to be separated from the print collection. If separations are made for the reason that the items are too large to fit neatly into regular library shelving, it might be more sensible to have a single over-size section where both print and nonprint items are shelved together.

It is probably not desirable to shelve paperbound trade books separately, and in most cases it may not be desirable to purchase them if hardbound versions are available. While the more fragile nature of paperbacks may cause some problems on the shelf, when they are used as supplementary textbooks rather than for pleasure reading, they should appear in their normal order in the collection. If a collection contains many teachers' manuals and workbooks in paper binding or spiral back, the inevitability of damage may have to be accepted, since binding costs are high and the materials have a limited life-span anyway.

Another category which might be shelved separately is the collection of bad examples of curriculum materials. Some people feel that intershelving undesirable material is dangerous since inexperienced students may not recognize it and use it in a classroom situation. Materials which have poor format, inaccuracies, poor writing, and unsatisfactory illustrations may need to be so labeled and taught for what they are--examples of poor evaluation and selection.

Standardized tests are usually collected on a selective basis. These are tests which have been tested extensively and for which norms have been established. These include psychological, attitudinal, achievement and intelligence tests. The publishers sometimes offer sample sets with instructions. Tests are usually supposed to be restricted to in-house use and cannot be copied. They are filed by author or publisher under the type of test. The test file may be limited if a more extensive collection is maintained in a centralized testing unit or in the psychology department on campus. Sometimes only the tests specifically requested by faculty are acquired. The file might include:

Diagnostic reading tests
Vocational interest tests
Adult basic education tests
Aptitude tests

Achievement tests
Test of mental maturity
Mental Ability tests
Comprehensive basic skills tests

Some centers report having ACT and CLEP tests but most prefer not to have them since there are greater security problems if they are included. Recent court decisions may make open access to tests compulsory and eliminate the special sign-up sheets and faculty permission slips now used in circulating tests in curriculum materials centers.

Circulation Services

It has been said that the results of the move of curriculum collections to the library were primarily reflected in an increase in circulation of materials to a broader clientele, longer loan periods, and greater numbers of materials allowed for check-out at one time. A basic philosophical question must be settled before loan policies are set, and the recommendations of the advisory committee and other related agencies and, if possible, a user study would all contribute toward making good policy decisions.

Some of the considerations which must be taken into account and discussed arise from the non-circulation policies which were common in the laboratory situation. Most materials used are not read from cover to cover or thoroughly viewed or listened to. The use is often selective and sometimes involves a comparison of several items. Some material must be used by all students in a class--a common condition during a children's literature course. When classes come to the center as a group, it is important that materials be there so that they can be examined as they are explained. If the center serving a regional community circulates materials, some patrons may drive miles to examine items, only to find them in circulation and not available. By its very nature the collection is made up of samples, and these samples should be available for examination at all times. Some centers do not lend off campus or on interlibrary loan. Others treat materials as they are treated in any library situation, i.e., most materials circulate, reference books and special collections do not, and fragile items cannot be borrowed on interlibrary loan. As part of the library, the center should have policies that are somewhat consistent with other library policies. This consistency will be expected by the users of the center and will be easier to manage. Some items, such as manuals which are used to teach materials production, may be needed at all times for consultation by people creating materials.

Some curriculum materials centers do not lend materials at all, but most centers located in libraries do circulate most materials under policies which vary widely, in type of borrower served, loan periods, and amount of material to be borrowed at one time. Some centers lend only to faculty, some only to student teachers, to education students, or to all students. It is common for curriculum centers to lend materials to teachers in the community, and sometimes they lend to any local borrower. The loan periods tend to vary according to the type of item borrowed.

An appropriate philosophy of circulation might be that the curriculum materials should conform to general library practice, with exceptions made which are similar to variations in circulation for other library collections. The exceptions might include:

1. Materials used by a whole class would not circulate during the semester or quarter when the course is offered, except on a reserve system basis with short loan periods.
2. Audiovisual and other fragile materials would not be lent on interlibrary loan.
3. Multimedia materials would not be lent for regular use in classes in public schools.
4. Caldecott and Newbery books would not circulate unless a duplicate were available for that purpose.
5. Textbooks would have a short loan period--five days or one week.
6. Tests would be used only within the center or for class demonstrations, with permission of the faculty member teaching the class.

The practice of limiting circulation to the education faculty and students does not seem to be common in recent years. Some materials are used in other classes on campus. The history and women's studies departments have courses on the history of childhood which require that students use the children's book collection as original research material on contemporary attitudes toward children. Art appreciation classes may use slide or picture collections.

Flandro felt that the curriculum center should not circulate materials as freely as other library departments and
that the items in the collection should not be lent to public
school classes unless they were being tested and evaluated
on a class. [5] However, the curriculum center is not meant
to be a museum and may not be able to serve its function
as an examination center if it does not use the circulation
privilege as a major way to encourage people to come to the
center and use its services. Full service in one situation
may involve a group of teachers serving as a curriculum
committee who come to the center to examine materials for
a specific grade and subject; spend several sessions meeting
and discussing various materials in a conference room; borrow and test some materials on classes of children; and
leave with citations, ideas, and resources which they can use
to complete a course of study. Advice and consultation by
the librarian should be provided as needed, browsing of the
collection encouraged, and appropriate referrals made to
other resources available on campus. Circulation policies
should also include loans to faculty who teach classes off-
campus so that extension students have some ideas of what
is available in the curriculum materials center. There will
always be some things which cannot be lent. Among things
which Arnett found were not circulated were tests, programmed textbooks, student-made units, reference books and
resource units. [6]

Some curriculum centers even serve town children,
although this necessitates maintaining a reserve collection
for the children's literature classes. Allowing children to
use the collection may be more of an advantage than a disadvantage if the traffic is fairly limited. Certainly, allowing
many children into an area where serious research is being
done can be disrupting. However, the chance to collect
evaluations of the material directly from the ultimate user
can improve the ability of the professional selector of materials and the practice can provide a population for student
research. The decision whether to allow use by children
would have to depend on its effect on the primary clientele.
It is possible to have two copies of prize-winning books so
that use by children will not interfere with academic classroom use.

The curriculum materials center now often handles its
own circulation even if the center is located physically in the
main library building. This is because there are more restrictions on many materials than in the main library collec-

tion. Overnight, two-hour, or one-day loan periods are
more closely related to the policies of the library reserve
service than to regular circulation. Without an automated
system, the main circulation department's personnel are unlikely to be aware of all the special types of curriculum
materials and their varied loan periods. Limitation on numbers of items borrowed are also common, and circulation of
vertical file and picture materials may require the use of
special envelopes and containers. If an automated circulation
system permits variations in loan periods by both type of
material and type of patron, and the center is located in the
main library, the circulation function could be handled entirely
by the library's circulation department. One library has its
ERIC microfiche entered into the circulation system. This
practice permits a keyword-in-title search on the system to
locate curriculum guides and is useful for the curriculum
reference service.

The handling of fines and overdues should conform as
closely as possible to general library practice. This can
easily be accomplished where an automated circulation system
is used and is easier to manage if standard practices are
followed and users expect the same rules through the library
system.

Reference Service

Anderson, in Principles and Practices of Curriculum
Development, said that the point of view of professional educators was that:

> Consultant services are needed to assist teachers
> and students in the utilization of the curriculum
> laboratory. Consultants ought to be trained as
> teachers, not as librarians. The system of
> filing the materials is somewhat mechanical and
> routine and can be readily learned, but the in-
> sights and understandings that are necessary for
> assisting teachers to find materials for curricu-
> lum study are far more important. [7]

This attitude, which misunderstands the role of reference librarians, assumes that the librarian does not have a subject
master's or doctoral degree in the field of education, and has
sometimes resulted in the duplication of some of the curriculum center's functions in the education department. Many of

the services of a well supplied center in a California library have been duplicated by a learning resources laboratory in the education department.   There is no obvious reason for this duplication since both centers seem to be functioning effectively a block or two apart on a relatively small campus, but this type of duplication seems generally to be the result of misconceptions about the type of reference and consultation service which is available in a library-based curriculum materials center.

If the curriculum materials center is not to be duplicated or to become a dead storage area, attention must be given to the user's needs for ease of access in organization, good reference service, continuous efforts to create circulation procedures which are as generous and flexible as possible, and continual anticipation of the future needs of the clientele. The professional staff should be encouraging, responsive in meeting individual needs, creative in preparing an environment for learning, and knowledgeable in relating the materials to the content of courses.   Reference services should include:

1. Locating information in the collection
2. Teaching evaluation and selection of materials
3. Introducing the various types of special education materials and their use in curriculum development
4. Teaching the use of reference books
5. Keeping faculty aware of new materials of interest in their classes.

In order to provide needed service and to teach students that the curriculum collection is merely a sample of the materials available to teachers, a good reference collection should include:

1. Bibliographies and sources for purchase
2. Reference books common to school media centers
3. Basic how-to-do-it books in frequent use for consultation in media production courses available in the center, even if these are duplicated in the professional education collection
4. Miscellaneous resources in support of the service of the center.

This last group might contain such items as Juniorplots: A

Book Talk for Teachers and Librarians by John T. Gillespie and Diana L. Lembo (New York: Bowker, 1967) and More Juniorplots: A Guide for Teachers and Librarians by John T. Gillespie (New York: Bowker, 1977), which include information for book talks and summaries of plots of books for children and young people.

The choice of indexes and bibliographies will depend on what other campus needs might dictate their inclusion in the main or a subject reference collection. Because the NICEM indexes are often kept in the main reference department in support of general media services on campus, the curriculum collection is seldom the location for the latest editions of these indexes. Instead, superseded editions are transferred there so that the curriculum center personnel can demonstrate these indexes and teach education students about NICEM before making referrals to the main reference room for recent entries. Often the students do not need the actual indexed information but are required by class assignments to identify and examine the NICEM indexes.

MacVean lists some of the reference questions frequently asked. These questions are not unusual in any curriculum center:

> Which of the reading series have special help for the poor readers? Where can I find enrichment materials for my superior readers? How does the textbook adoptions system work? What is the core curriculum?[8]

Other questions might include: Where can I find an example of a policy on selecting textbooks? Where can I find some projects that elementary school students can use for a science fair? Are there books which have the English and Spanish text on adjacent pages? Such questions require that a knowledgeable reference staff be present during all peak use hours and that well-trained students be available during low-use hours such as 10 p.m. to midnight. If this minimal staffing is not possible, the library will need to arrange for the transfer of appropriate library staff from other areas. When only a student assistant is on duty, a librarian may assume supervisory and on-call reference services in addition to work in some other nearby service area. During the summer when many teachers are taking courses on campus, extra service personnel should be available.

One of the advantages of locating the curriculum materials collection in the library is that it encourages better interlibrary loan service, both to local users and to other libraries. Now that an increasing number of state publications are showing up in OCLC, some of the more interesting but elusive curriculum guides may be available for loan.

A Public Relations Program

As a result of his study of curriculum laboratories, Flandro found four general rules for success: (1) involve all the faculty in using and selecting materials, (2) make materials easily and readily available, (3) make administration simple and informal, and (4) publicize materials and services.[9] This last requirement, "to publicize materials and services," requires a commitment to a continuing public relations program by the staff servicing the curriculum collection.

Work with the faculty of the teacher education program may form the background for publicizing the center to its primary users, the students in education courses. Some tasks which would contribute to cooperation with the faculty would be:

1. To prepare a video-tape or slide-tape program on the center for use in classes
2. To furnish materials for bulletin boards and displays
3. To encourage teachers of methods and curriculum courses to hold a class in the center's conference room where samples of materials could be on display and be discussed
4. When the college of education holds a publishers' exhibit, to cooperate and perhaps take a leadership role if requested to do so
5. To assist the college or department in holding workshops on evaluation of materials or curriculum construction and to hold such workshops for school library media personnel and other librarians
6. If the curriculum materials center is located near education classes where trucks can travel to classrooms, to remind faculty that they may borrow materials for classroom use and demonstration
7. To include the curriculum center as part of a

general freshman orientation program
8. To give lectures to classes which may need to use the center's collection
9. To insure that the collection is represented in the library's card catalog and circulation data base
10. To provide tours or demonstrations to participants in any conferences or meetings held by the college or department of education
11. To circulate reports on the growth of the collection
12. To circulate reports on user satisfaction studies.

The curriculum center librarians should also be aware that other classes on campus may need to use the collection. Children's book collections are sometimes used not only for the courses in professional education but also for story-telling classes in theatre arts or for a history of childhood course in the history department. Special lectures need to be prepared for these groups, each offering an approach to children's literature which is geared to the use made of it by the class.

When no conference room is available, shelving may be arranged to create a space dedicated for group lectures and demonstrations of materials. If periodical display shelving is used, the materials to be demonstrated can be displayed on the slanting shelves so that students can examine them as part of an orientation to the curriculum center.

The curriculum laboratory at George Peabody College, as early as the 1930s, dedicated an important part of its service to the holding of workshops on curriculum construction for teachers in Florida and Virginia and, later, other states as well. With the change in emphasis to a more limited role of providing advice and assistance on curriculum construction and provision of sample materials, it is doubtful whether the kind of outreach activity provided by Peabody is ever offered to teachers by academic library curriculum centers today. The academic centers should, however, be offering some services and these need to be publicized through an active public relations program.

Some public relations activities which could increase the use of the center by making community teachers and researchers more aware of services might include:

1. Inviting professional associations or groups of teachers and school media specialists to hold one of their meetings in the center
2. Inviting teachers to special previews of new materials
3. Holding publishers' demonstrations under joint sponsorship with other appropriate agencies in the college or university and with local schools
4. Seeking opportunities to deliver talks about the center to groups of teachers
5. Arranging cooperative publicity programs with school library media center directors; these could be built around Children's Book Week, National Library Week, or some local event.
6. Periodically providing lists of media by form to school library media personnel
7. Providing space for regular display programs which can be used for subject displays or for display of one type of product and sending notices of the display to local schools
8. If appropriate, insuring that the materials are entered into the OCLC system for better availability on interlibrary loan.

Because some school systems have set aside time specifically for continuing education for teachers and school media center personnel, it is a good idea to contact local administrators and offer the services of the center for a program on instructional materials.

Another way for the director and professional staff of the center to publicize the curriculum materials center and make its collections better known is through research, publication, and contacts with colleagues in professional associations.

St. Cyr's study of curriculum collections found that teachers had very little interest in research publications from the center but that they expressed a desire for a bulletin which would let them know what materials the center had which might be valuable to them.[10] MacVean reported that education faculty thought the curriculum center should publish "reproductions of some of the best work of students in methods classes for general distribution," and "lists of resource units."[11] Much of the publication effort of curriculum materials centers seems to go into the preparation of bibliographies and guides which help students identify and locate materials on a particular subject or for a particular purpose. This is similar to practices in other library departments. Unfortunately, these publications may not be distributed widely outside of the centers.

A very useful guide describing the search strategy for preparing a teaching unit has been written by Urania Gluesing, the Curriculum Librarian at San Francisco State University. This guide not only leads the student to the types of materials needed but also refers the researcher to other resources in the library, the campus, and the community (see Figures 6 and 7).

The sharing of such publications among curriculum libraries in different institutions could encourage the preparation of more materials to assist users and to publicize services available to outsiders. Flandro reported that there was also little contact between curriculum laboratories.[12] An exception occurred in recent years when a meeting of California curriculum librarians was held at Sacramento State University. A Curriculum Committee of the Education and Behavioral Sciences Section of the Association of College and Research Libraries meets at each conference of the American Library Association. This committee and its observers sometimes serve as a good communication channel for curriculum librarians who attend ALA conferences. Many curriculum materials librarians obtain their only professional interaction with colleagues in school library media centers, whose concerns may be only somewhat similar. The professional associations and the professional journals need to give more attention to this particular aspect of academic library service.

Audiovisual Services

Students, faculty, and community users of the curriculum materials center ask for advice on audio recording techniques, photographic techniques, graphic arts, sources for supplies, sources of repairs on equipment, and for photocopy and printing service. Just as there are special criteria to be considered when selecting nonprint media, there are also special service considerations. Is the equipment available to use the media properly? Does the unit come with satisfactory boxing or packaging, or can this be

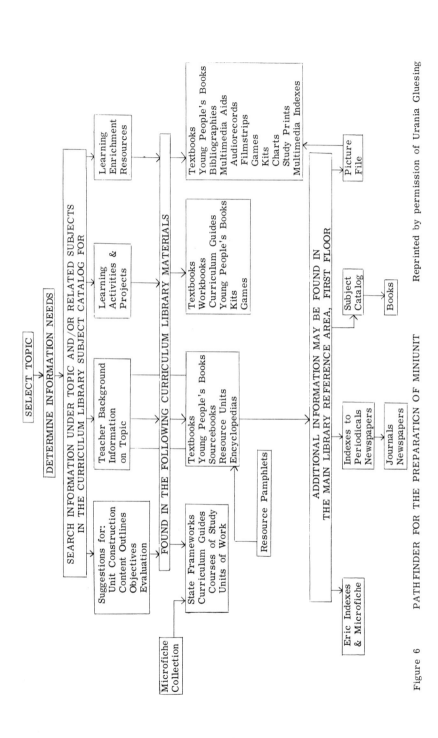

SELECT TOPIC

DETERMINE INFORMATION NEEDS

SEARCH INFORMATION UNDER TOPIC AND/OR RELATED SUBJECTS
IN THE CURRICULUM LIBRARY SUBJECT CATALOG FOR

Suggestions for:
Unit Construction
Content Outlines
Objectives
Evaluation

Teacher Background
Information
on Topic

Learning
Activities &
Projects

Learning
Enrichment
Resources

FOUND IN THE FOLLOWING CURRICULUM LIBRARY MATERIALS

State Frameworks
Curriculum Guides
Courses of Study
Units of Work

Textbooks
Young People's Books
Sourcebooks
Resource Units
Encyclopedias

Textbooks
Workbooks
Curriculum Guides
Young People's Books
Kits
Games

Textbooks
Young People's Books
Bibliographies
Multimedia Aids
Audiorecords
Filmstrips
Games
Kits
Charts
Study Prints
Multimedia Indexes

Resource Pamphlets

Microfiche
Collection

ADDITIONAL INFORMATION MAY BE FOUND IN
THE MAIN LIBRARY REFERENCE AREA, FIRST FLOOR

Eric Indexes
& Microfiche

Indexes to
Periodicals
Newspapers

Journals
Newspapers

Subject
Catalog

Books

Picture
File

Figure 6   PATHFINDER FOR THE PREPARATION OF MINIUNIT

Reprinted by permission of Urania Gluesing

Figure 7

San Francisco State University
J. Paul Leonard Library
Curriculum Library

Prepared by Urania Gluesing, Curriculum Librarian

Pathfinder for the Preparation of a Mini-unit

1. Select a topic

2. Determine information needs

3. Search information in the Curriculum Library's subject
   catalog under the topic and/or related subjects for:
   a. Suggestions for unit construction including content out-
      lines, concepts and main ideas, objectives, teaching
      strategies and evaluation. These are found in state
      frameworks, also in curriculum guides which include
      courses of study and units of work. The microfiche
      collection of curriculum guides (not listed in the card
      catalog) is also a source of helpful suggestions.
      Teacher's editions or teacher's guides to textbooks
      offer innovative teaching techniques.
   b. Teacher background information on the topic. Useful
      resources include textbooks, young people's books
      sourcebooks, resource units, encyclopedias and re-
      source pamphlets.
   c. Learning activities, projects. Textbooks, workbooks,
      curriculum guides, activity collections, young people's
      books, kits and games are good sources.
   d. Learning enrichment resources for the regular class-
      room and mainstreaming. Bibliographies and reading
      lists in a unit, related to the topic explored, may in-
      clude basic and supplemental learning aids such as
      textbooks, children's library books, and multimedia
      aids as audiorecords, filmstrips, games, kits, charts,
      study prints. Subject bibliographies of children's liter-
      ature and classroom materials and multimedia indexes
      are helpful supplements to the Curriculum Library's
      card catalog in identifying specific titles on a topic.

4. Additional materials located in the reference area on the
   first floor of the main library:
   a. Teacher background information: The subject catalog

may list books that include information on the topic.
Newspaper indexes and periodical indexes to journal
articles related to the topic, are also useful, especially if the topic is about a current issue.
   b. The ERIC indexes and microfiche collection for ideas
   on unit preparation, particularly for innovative approaches.
   c. The picture file of mounted photographs and illustrations serves as a source of effective visual aids on
   many school subjects.

5. The Audiovisual Center on the ground floor of the Library building provides films, filmstrips, videocassettes,
   audiotapes and slides on curriculum-related subjects.
   Some of these media are available for preview in the
   Student Learning Center on the fourth floor (Room 432)
   of the Library.

6. Off-campus learning resources identified in the community
   and related to the selected topic.

*   *   *

achieved in some other way? Can people be interested in
using the item? Does it do something unique?

   The librarian whose course work has not emphasized
the managing of nonprint materials may want to brush up by
reading and study on the subject. Follett Library Book Company puts out three sound filmstrips designed to teach children to operate various pieces of equipment, but these filmstrips also have an adult audience in mind and can be used
to train staff. Many useful books on managing nonprint media
are readily accessible, including:

> Hicks, Warren G. and Alma M. Tillin. Managing
> Multimedia Libraries. (New York: Bowker,
> 1977).
> Hicks, Warren B. and Alma M. Tillin. Develop-
> ing Multi-Media Libraries. (New York:
> Bowker, 1970).
> Gillespie, John T. and Diana L. Spirt. Creating
> a School Media Program. (New York: Bow-
> ker, 1973).
> Nadler, Myra, ed. How to Start an Audiovisual
> Collection. (Metuchen, N. J.: Scarecrow
> Press, 1978).

Sive, Mary Robinson. Selecting Instructional Media. (Littleton, Colo.: Libraries Unlimited, 1978).

These titles cover the handling of multimedia in a variety of library situations and include definitions of terms, practical instruction, and general sources for materials and equipment.

Access to closed circuit television and VTR or disc equipment is not universal in curriculum centers. Fortunately, the curriculum center is frequently housed adjacent to a media center or a media production center which provides such equipment and which is used by the curriculum staff in advising students and others in the use of these media forms. This physical proximity has advantages since it sets up a good liaison and a desirable cooperation between the two staffs.

Where the two services are combined, there are some problems in trying to integrate the multimedia services of the curriculum materials laboratory with the general audiovisual services of the library. The library's general service is often designed strictly for individual use, primarily in response to assignments of materials by faculty to supplement classroom work. With this type of reserve service on media materials, the student user seeks a specific item and uses it on a piece of equipment designed for individual projection or listening in a self-service situation. This service differs drastically from the service to student teachers, community teachers, and others who may be reviewing a wide variety of materials on equipment designed for either individual or group use. Teachers may have created a multimedia program, for example, and wish to test the results for distance projection as well as individual use situations; in such cases they will need a wider variety of equipment and facilities.

Problems can result if the curriculum center lends equipment to a student teacher for course work in practice teaching but refuses to lend it to other students for their regular college coursework. Lending equipment requires greater duplication and spending more in maintenance, repairs, and supplies. This may be justified where the student's education requires an opportunity to practice teach with a certain form of material, but may not be reasonable financially to provide this option to all university students

who need equipment only to review specific items. In choosing video and audio equipment some thought should be given
to compatibility with home recording and playing equipment
because this makes previewing easier and can contribute to
longer life of the equipment in the center. Counterbalancing
this, of course, is the possible increase in thefts of the com-
patible software.

When the two types of library media services are combined, there may also be differences in the way materials
are organized. Materials for general support of the regular
college curriculum should be handled in the same way as
print materials, so that students do not have to learn unnecessary variations in the classification scheme. When audiovisual materials are used in the course reserve situation,
students will often follow the same practice as with printed
materials; they will ask for the item by course number or by
instructor's name. If access is by self-service, the media
may be sorted on the shelf in either of these ways. If materials are handed out by library personnel, indexes by producer, title, course number, or instructor's name may be
provided and materials stored in their normal classification
order. In the curriculum collection, it is important that
media be kept in their normal curriculum classification system where they will be found by general subject, grade level,
and specific subject, preferably intershelved with printed materials in the same categories. The few times when the material will be used in a reserve type of situation, it can be
handled almost on an individual basis at the circulation desk.

Some institutions include the general audiovisual service in the curriculum center for reasons of expediency; only
one set of personnel needs to be trained to know and service
multimedia materials and equipment, equipment is centralized
for security and repairs, and only one space must be prepared with special wiring and cables.

Where the general library has the responsibility for
the media services to the instructional programs of the university or college and is providing the equipment and media
for use in all college classrooms, the multimedia services in
the curriculum center become a small subset of a large and
complex program. In this case the relationship of the curriculum materials center will be similar to what it has been to
campus audiovisual services in other institutions. The center
becomes a patron of the general service area, borrowing special equipment, obtaining repair services and supplies, and
seeking expert technical assistance as necessary.

Maintaining equipment in good condition is a two-level process: 1) regular cleaning, replacing of bulbs and general minor repairs, and 2) major repairs and replacement of parts. The first is a management function of the center, while the second should be done in whatever unit of the total system has the technicians trained to do such work. This is usually not the library-based curriculum collection area. It may be in the library media service department or in a campus media center. The campus media center may actually have the equipment in its inventory but on permanent loan to the curriculum materials center. The campus center may replace or exchange cquipment as damage or wear dictates.

Some repairs are handled under maintenance contracts with the vendor or manufacturer of the equipment. This is often the most satisfactory practice on expensive or complex items since the technicians are then usually factory-trained and a stock of replacement parts is maintained at all times.

Regular care and maintenance of both equipment and media require at least a limited number of activities, including: 1) provision for splicers for all kinds of film and tape, record washers, earphone sterilizers and other maintenance equipment; and 2) keeping the supplies needed for repair and cleaning of materials and equipment. Library supply houses sell splicing tape for film and audio tape, tape head cleaners for video and audio cassettes, static free cleaning cloth, anti-static cleaning fluids, film cleaner and suitable swabs and brushes. Special kits of supplies are available from library and media supply catalogs which are designed to be used in the care of specific media forms such as video cassette recorders, microforms, or for multimedia.

Regular daily maintenance of cleaning screens, dusting equipment and tables, using anti-static spray on carpets, and examining materials upon return from circulation will prevent many problems. Plastic storage containers protect video tape from heat and humidity. [13]

Renting 16mm film

Most curriculum centers do not have 16mm films. The expense of building and keeping such a collection current is usually far beyond the center's materials budget. In 1957 Flandro found that of 65 centers studied, 31 had virtually no sharing of materials with the campus media center where

16mm film might be available, 11 had very little sharing, and only 23 had any history of extensive sharing.[14] This format is still probably not one that can be easily obtained from another campus agency.

The curriculum center must rely on other agencies for 16mm film--usually rentals from off-campus sources. While one or two sample films may be kept on hand for the purpose of teaching students to use 16mm equipment, most of the need for this size of film is for use in classes where practice teaching is going on. If the student teacher needs to use 16mm film or if a teacher in the community asks for sources for this type of film, the curriculum librarian may make referrals to:

1. School or school district collections
2. State library sources
3. Commercial sources for purchase
4. Government sources
5. Advertising materials from business and industry
6. Collections in colleges and universities providing rental services.

School and school district centers are often in the same position as the curriculum center. Their 16mm collections are often limited to a few films which are used so often that purchase is less expensive than rental.

In many cases state library 16mm film collections are also not available for use in schools or by student teachers for classroom use, but are restricted to out-of-school public programs. The only benefit to local teachers or student teachers may be for use in after-school public programs such as Girl Scout meetings or PTA meetings.

Commercial sources for purchase are extensive. Every curriculum center should have access to the NICEM Index to 16mm Educational Films, a three-volume set now in its seventh edition. If the center does not have all of the NICEM indexes, the patrons can be referred to the general library reference department for use of these tools.

In most cases, the curriculum center can best serve its clientele by referring them to sources for rental of 16mm film. Rental of film is not easy, however. The sources for the best films are often overwhelmed with the demand, so that a long lead time for reservations of film is required. Delivery costs and delays are frustrating and rental fees are sometimes quite high.

Business and government sources are often the least expensive, but they must be used with caution since, understandably, they present the message of their producers. The Educator's Guide to Free Films indexes business-produced films and as an annual publication keeps an up-to-date list. The National Union Catalog: Films and Other Materials for Projection, 1973-78 and other Library of Congress publications can help in identifying films. Documentary Film Classics Produced by the United States Government is an example of the National Audio Visual Center's program, which provides access to more than 12,000 non-book sources. This listing includes films which can be purchased in 16mm or in video cassette and may often be rented in either format. Containing such documentary materials as the Pare Lorentz classics of the 1930s' depression and Frank Capra's films of World War II, the list warns that there may be delays on rentals and asks for a choice of rental dates. Unfortunately, this is a choice that student teachers do not always have.

Curriculum center personnel will send most people to a university in their own state which specializes in film rentals. Such institutions as the University of Southern California and Indiana University have excellent catalogs of films available for rent. To avoid mail delays the curriculum center will make many referrals to centers in its own state or a nearby state.

Evaluating the Services

As in any other library program, in the curriculum materials center a regular ongoing evaluation should take place. Some of the means of evaluating the performance of the center can come from:

1. Examining statistics on new materials
2. Examining statistics on circulation, reference and in-house use
3. Evaluating staff development
4. Researching the effects of changes or new service added
5. Measuring costs of the center and the cost of outside support from technical service units

CURRICULUM MATERIALS CENTER

Statistics for _____, 19__

Reference Questions
    Directional   _____
    Brief reference   _____
    Research   _____
    Telephone   _____
    Total   _____

Circulation	In house			Outside		
	Student	Faculty	Other	Student	Faculty	Other
Books	_____	_____	_____	_____	_____	_____
Serials	_____	_____	_____	_____	_____	_____
Vertical file	_____	_____	_____	_____	_____	_____
Curriculum guides	_____	_____	_____	_____	_____	_____
Textbooks	_____	_____	_____	_____	_____	_____
Tests	_____	_____	_____	_____	_____	_____
Nonprint media	_____	_____	_____	_____	_____	_____
Equipment	_____	_____	_____	_____	_____	_____
Picture file	_____	_____	_____	_____	_____	_____
Totals	_____	_____	_____	_____	_____	_____
Grand Total	_____			_____		

Tours	Number of classes, groups	Number of students, individuals
Orientation tours	_____	_____
Lectures	_____	_____
Materials presentations	_____	_____
Group work	_____	_____
Visitors	_____	_____
Totals	_____	_____

Bibliographies prepared   _____
Displays prepared   _____

Figure 8

6. User studies
7. Document delivery studies.

For evaluation purposes, a statistics sheet might be prepared for gathering the needed quantitative data. Figure 8 is an example of such a statistical report. Statistics should reflect some of the questions asked in the guidelines of the NCATE Standards. Reference statistics could offer some evidence for the questions: "What information shows that the center is directed by personnel who are knowledgeable about instructional media and materials?" Circulation and reference statistics could help to answer: "What information indicates that the center is available to and used by: a. Students? b. Teacher education faculty members?"[15] Statistics on the growth of the collection will probably be collected as part of the function of checking in new material in the acquisitions departments of the library. If some materials come directly to the center, it is important that a reporting procedure be set up to include these items in the library's statistics on collection growth.

User studies may measure the perceptions of the library's clientele about the adequacy of the services and collections provided. Document delivery studies turn out often to reflect general user satisfaction, since failure to produce a specific document may not be a failure in the eyes of the patron if another document deemed just as good has been provided.

John G. Church developed a questionnaire for evaluating curriculum laboratories. Some of his criteria are appropriate for the present centers based in academic libraries where services emphasize the provision of materials and reference help. Under the objectives of the center, Church included such criteria as 1) the teaching of locating, evaluating and using audiovisual aids, and other curriculum materials, 2) help in learning to locate diagnostic and developmental education aids, 3) keeping the center's collection in tune with the latest changes in the education program, 4) providing materials for individual instruction. Evaluation questions on these criteria would be appropriate for measuring the services of the academic library's curriculum collection.[16]

Other areas of Church's evaluation instrument included several criteria under such topics as the director, the professional staff, the physical plant, the materials, the classification, the finances and administrative relationship, activities, and policies for users. Church's evaluation form, which includes both a scale indicating whether the question applies and a separate scale for the degree of adequacy, could be used directly or could serve as a basis for modifications which would better measure the effectiveness of a library-based curriculum center. The best thing about Church's instrument is that the adequacy of services can be evaluated in the context of the facilities, budget, administration, and personnel available to provide them. It is, therefore, a good self-evaluation instrument.[17]

In actual practice, evaluating the staffing of a curriculum collection is very complex. Variations in staff size do not always seem to correlate with the services offered. For example, some collections which have no dedicated full-time staff seem to provide good service because they are located near or adjacent to other supporting services such as educational reference or the library's media center. Centers which do all or nearly all of their own processing vary widely in staff size. There seems to be no recent evidence on the correlation between size of staff and use of a center, and the variables would make it hard to prove whether a larger staff increases volume of use or whether amount of use is more a product of the types and variety of service or the distance from other similar services. Clearly, good management of a center necessitates identifying costs and evaluating services before making decisions on the amount and type of staff needed.

Keeping the Collection Current

One way that curriculum materials differ from most of the library's collections is in their fairly temporary nature. Heidbreder and Swanker, writing about these materials in educational media evaluation centers, said that they would need to be kept only eighteen months to two years.[18] St. Cyr's research indicated that "old materials should be discarded unless their content has some particular value.[19] Some publishers actually ask that older editions be removed as new ones appear. Most curriculum centers do not contain much material over ten years old.

Various studies done over the years and the centers visited by the author indicate that most centers failed to weed the collection as often as the staff thought it was necessary.

A wide variety of practices include weeding done once per quarter or semester, semi-annually, as editions are revised, annually, once in three or four years, and "as needed." Limited personnel is the usual reason given for a lack of a regular weeding program. However, all curriculum materials centers seem to withdraw old materials as new editions appear or as outdated materials come to the attention of the staff.

Withdrawal practices vary not only among different institutions but also among different types of materials in the same collection. The pattern for withdrawal may be one or more of the following practices:

1. Comparison with standard bibliographies
2. According to standards suggested by various professional organizations or research reports
3. According to copyright or publication date
4. Continual evaluation as materials are used
5. As reviewed by faculty or an advisory committee
6. In a general inventory on a regular basis
7. By category, such as all out-of-print textbooks
8. As new titles or editions replace existing items
9. Because of damage or local duplication.

St. Cyr found that a significant minority of the School of Education professors at Michigan felt that: "the Center should have old materials available in some way for research purposes."[20] Johnson reported that "The director at UCLA discarded many older materials, only to discover too late that some of those materials were much sought after."[21] The practice of keeping older materials is quite common. Johnson found five institutions doing this.[22]

Older materials, if kept, should be shelved separately. Otherwise, students may be misled into using outdated educational methods and theories. A curriculum materials center can create a separate historical collection made up of superseded textbooks, outdated methodology, old pictures and children's books. These materials may be used in history of education courses, for courses in history of childhood, or for other social and intellectual history research. Some curriculum centers have a fairly good collection of fiction and nonfiction trade books, used to supplement the textbook in classroom work. While some materials of this kind are classics which have a long life, others are outdated almost as quickly as instructional media and textbooks and should be weeded from the active collection.

It would seem appropriate that older materials which are to be retained be transferred as a unit to the library's general research collection or that they become a special collection in a department with other special collections. It is important that a decision be made about keeping locally produced curriculum guides and courses of study. Probably only one institution in each area needs to keep them as part of the record of local education. A decision should also be made whether to keep only those of the local school system or all of those in the county or state.

Space is always a consideration when making withdrawals. Some curriculum center directors admit that they keep the historical collection to insure that they do not lose space or shelving to other library purposes when they feel that it will be needed eventually for the center's primary purposes. Often, curriculum materials centers have not weeded the multimedia collections because these materials are fairly new and not so extensive as to require more space, and because a certain amount of continuous weeding is automatic as a result of loss of parts or deterioration from wear of certain forms of media.

There are alternatives to maintaining the outdated historical collection. Films can sometimes be transferred to other campus film collections. If the institution is a member of the Center for Research Libraries, CRL can be consulted to see if it wants any of the discarded materials transferred to its collections of textbooks, children's literature, or state publications. Before giving away any discarded materials, it is important to investigate what rules or legal requirements exist in those centers which are part of a state-supported institution. Strict rules may exist for the disposal of state property. The custom of putting withdrawn materials out for patrons to take, a fairly common practice, is questionable because incorrect or outdated information should not be offered to students who may not recognize it for what it is.

The Future

The development of curriculum centers has been a

gradual evolution as their management moved from colleges and departments of education to the academic libraries. At one time the U. S. Office of Education funded fifteen (originally 20) regional education laboratories to train teachers in curriculum construction. This emphasis changed somewhat as college courses supported by curriculum materials collections provided the instruction to new teachers.[23] Education programs in institutions of higher education are in a transitional stage and curriculum materials centers must reflect changes as they occur. The collection at the University of California, Berkeley, has changed in its role as a result of the education program's increased concentration on research and higher education rather than the training of classroom teachers for elementary and secondary schools. Under such conditions the materials of a practical nature become less important.

In 1979, William Dean Taylor observed that an increase in state control was inevitable as a result of the placing of major control of federal funds at the state level. He felt that an important change occurred in the state's role when a California court decision in 1971 required that the states equalize education between rich and poor districts.[24] The Council of Chief State School Officers developed a policy to guide state education departments in their involvement with nonprint media in schools.[25] This type of responsibility, vested increasingly in state government, has raised some controversy about the control of education. Recent issues such as minimum competency examinations, educational voucher programs, increasing numbers of private schools, demands for accountability, taxpayer revolts, and increased activity by teachers' unions have put control into different levels of government and in other agencies. As a result of these activities teacher education may change and the supporting curriculum collections may also change. The increase in the number of private day schools may change the nature of some of the clientele which uses curriculum centers.

A study by Robert Heinrich and Kim Ebert, financed by the National Institute of Education (DHEW) in 1975, looked at the legal barriers which limit the use of educational technology, since the newer forms of technology, video and computer instruction, have been seen as a major instrument of change in education in the future. The limitations which the study covered were those which in effect apply to the substitution of technology for the teacher and address the use of educational technology as the basic instruction vehicle rather than as a supplement to the teacher/pupil interaction form of education. Heinrich and Ebert found that the legal areas which limit technology were: "certification of teachers, accreditation of programs, state aid to schools, and professional negotiations."[26] In an age of taxpayer revolt, competency testing, and fiscal accountability, some of these legal restrictions may be eased. The structure of schools, their financing, and the movement of children to schools rather than the movement of information and instruction to the child through technology may change and have a major effect on the form of curriculum aids and information and how they will be handled. Curriculum center professionals should be involved in studying the direction in which education is going, keep abreast of the patterns of change occurring in professional education programs, and observe the activities of professional associations and commercial producers and publishers.

Heinrich and Ebert believe that "the teaching profession will have to come to terms with technological concepts and realize that increased productivity is the best route to real salary increases."[27] If teachers rely increasingly on more sophisticated technology for an increase in productivity, the role of curriculum materials centers will focus more on the provision of equipment and programs which will teach education students to use the technologies being developed.

Libraries which support a center will need to face the increased costs involved in supplying instruction, sample programs, and additional equipment that will assist the college faculty who prepare the teacher to make maximum use of the new media. Those centers which now do not have computer terminals or video disc equipment may face changes which are drastic financially as well as educationally. Colleges of education will be severely handicapped if the curriculum materials centers do not keep up with the changes in educational practices.

In the past, the wealth of research on curriculum materials centers has not always been made readily available to the practitioners in the field. Good developments in one center have not necessarily spread to other centers and librarians sometimes struggle alone with problems which are common to all curriculum collections. In a period of rapid change it is important to establish good information networks among the people responsible for maintaining curriculum materials collections in academic libraries.

The Education and Behavioral Sciences Section of the Association of College and Research Libraries has a Curriculum Materials Committee which is working on a statement of concerns about the administration of curriculum materials. It is expected that recommendations will be made to the Section that will offer guidelines to the people involved in managing such collections. It is hoped that these recommendations will look to the future as well as to existing practices. The results will also be more effective if some provision is made for greater professional interaction among the librarians responsible for the academic library curriculum collections.

NOTES

[1] Francis L. Drag, "Curriculum Laboratories in the United States" (Doctoral Dissertation, Stanford University, 1946), p. 96.

[2] Donald S. MacVean, "A Study of Curriculum Laboratories in Midwestern Teacher Training Institutions" (Doctoral Dissertation, University of Michigan, 1958), p. 105.

[3] Harold F. Smith and Charles Gardner, "Curriculum Materials in the Teachers College Library," College and Research Libraries 17 (July, 1956): 313.

[4] Helen Mae Arnett, "Accessibility of Instructional Materials with Implications for the Organization of Curriculum Laboratories" (Doctoral Dissertation, Western Reserve University, 1965), p. 139.

[5] Royce P. Flandro, "Curriculum Laboratories in Colleges of Teacher Education" (Doctoral Dissertation, Indiana University, 1957), p. 194.

[6] Arnett, "Accessibility of Instructional Materials," p. 138.

[7] Vernon Ellsworth Anderson, Principles and Procedures of Curriculum Improvement, 2nd ed. (New York: Ronald Press, 1965), p. 346.

[8] Donald S. MacVean, "Report of an Evaluation of Curriculum Laboratory Services in a Teachers College," Journal of Educational Research 53 (May, 1960): 344.

182 / Managing Curriculum Materials

9Flandro, "Curriculum Laboratories," p. 161.

[10]Carol Ruth St. Cyr, "Present and Potential Users of the University of Michigan Curriculum Materials Center" (Doctoral Dissertation, University of Michigan, 1955), p. 82.

[11]MacVean, "Report of an Evaluation," p. 343.

[12]Flandro, "Curriculum Laboratories," p. 148.

[13]Leon L. Drolet, Jr., "Software: The Key to a Successful Video Program," American Libraries 10 (December, 1979): 669.

[14]Flandro, "Curriculum Laboratories," p. 122.

[15]National Council for the Accreditation of Teacher Education, Standards for Accreditation of Teacher Education (Washington, D.C.: National Association for the Accreditation of Teacher Education, 1979), p. 25.

[16]John Gideon Church, "The Development of Criteria for Evaluating Curriculum Laboratories in Teacher Education Institutions" (Doctoral Dissertation, University of Utah, 1957), p. 112.

[17]Ibid., pp. 115-126.

[18]M. Ann Heidbreder and Esther Swanker, "Project: A Book Examination Center," Library Journal 4 (February 15, 1966): 1032.

[19]St. Cyr, "Present and Potential Users," p. 84.

[20]Ibid., p. 85.

[21]Harlan R. Johnson, "The Curriculum Materials Center: A Study of Policies and Practices" (Doctoral Dissertation, Northern Arizona University, 1973), p. 19.

[22]Ibid., p. 36.

[23]Robert F. Mager and Peter Pipe, Teacher Training Projects of the Regional Education Laboratories (Los Altos, California: Mager Associates, 1969), p. 34.

[24]William Dean Taylor, "Instructional Nonprint Media Pro-

grams of State Education Agencies" (Doctoral Dissertation, Indiana University, 1978), p. 8.

[25]Ibid., p. 13.

[26]Robert Heinrich and Kim Ebert, "Legal Barriers to Educa-
tional Technology and Instructional Productivity: Final
Report, " (ED 124 118) U.S. Department of Health,
Education and Welfare, National Institute of Education,
Program of Productivity and Technology, Washington,
D.C., May 1976, p. 7.

[27]Ibid., p. 9.

APPENDIX A

CURRICULUM MATERIALS CENTERS VISITED

While no effort was made to do extensive research replicating the results of previous research, visits were made to curriculum materials centers to survey present practices. The visits were used as a means of evaluating previous research appearing in theses and dissertations in the field of professional education, and check whether conclusions appearing in published research were still valid and being applied in the management of instructional materials collections in academic libraries. The interview instrument used was designed to: 1) identify the classification schemes used for organizing materials, with special attention to ephemeral areas such as picture files, curriculum guides, courses of study, unit and test files; 2) analyze the relationships with other supporting agencies on the campus or in the community; 3) examine the relationship between the library and production functions of the curriculum centers; and 4) study the types of instruction provided to professional education students by the personnel in the curriculum materials center. The information gathered was used to update and evaluate the recommendations from previous research.

The curriculum centers visited included:

Educational Resources Center
Syracuse University
Syracuse, New York
Jeryl Mitchell, Curriculum assistant

J. Paul Leonard Library
San Francisco State University
San Francisco, California
Urania Gluesing: Head, Curriculum Library

Learning Resources Center
New Mexico State University
Las Cruces, New Mexico
Frank Smith, Director

Memorial Library
State University of New York, Cortland
Cortland, New York
David Kreh: Librarian, Teaching Materials Center

Milne Library
State University of New York, Geneseo
Geneseo, New York
Barbara Clarke, Librarian, Curriculum Resources Center

Milne Library
State University of New York, Oneonta
Oneonta, New York
Leora Lucas, Teaching Materials Department

Rubin Salazar Library
Sonoma State University
Rohnert Park, California
Barbara Biebush: Education Reference Librarian

University Library
New Mexico State University
Las Cruces, New Mexico
Christine Buder: Special Collections Librarian

Educational Media Center
Sacramento County Board of Education
Sacramento, California
Harlow Clarke: Director

University Library
Sacramento State University
Sacramento, California
Stan Frost: Education/Psychology Librarian

University Library
San Jose State University
San Jose, California
Jeff Paul: Media Services Department

APPENDIX B

INTERVIEW QUESTIONNAIRE

1) How are materials classified and organized for retrieval?

Classification
Card Catalog

Automated Circulation System
Shelflist
Publishers Catalog
Picture File
Curriculum guides
Learning Centers
Realia

2) What is your relationship with:

General Library

Education Library

Campus audio visual services (Teaching Aids, telecommunication, Listening Center. Photography service, photocopy service, etc., computer services)

Testing services

Laboratory school or preschool

Extension center and adult education

Reading and tutoring labs

Bookstore

Library School

187

3) What is your relationship to:

> State education department
> Public and private schools
> Other colleges and universities
> School curriculum committees
> Public libraries
> Commercial media (cable TV, etc.)

4) Does your center include production facilities to create:

> Print, posters, graphics
> Slides, filmstrip
> Film (Super 8, 16mm, filmloops)
> Television
>> Tapes
>> Cassettes
>> Disc
>> Cable linkage to classroom
>> Remote dial access
> Audio
>> Radio
>> Tape

5) Do you have an orientation and instruction program?

> Tours
> Lectures to methods classes
> Lectures to other classes
> Programs for community school personnel
> Workshops

APPENDIX C

LIBRARY BILL OF RIGHTS

The American Library Association affirms that all libraries are forums for information and ideas, and that the following basic policies should guide their services.

1. Books and other library sources should be provided for the interest, information, and enlightenment of all people of the community the library serves. Materials should not be excluded because of the origin, background, or views of those contributing to their creation.

2. Libraries should provide materials and information presenting all points of view on current and historical issues. Materials should not be proscribed or removed because of partisan or doctrinal disapproval.

3. Libraries should challenge censorship in the fulfillment of their responsibility to provide information and enlightenment.

4. Libraries should cooperate with all persons and groups concerned with resisting abridgment of free expression and free access to ideas.

5. A person's right to use a library should not be denied or abridged because of origin, age, background, or views.

6. Libraries which make exhibit spaces and meeting rooms available to the public they serve should make such facilities available on an equitable basis, regardless of the beliefs or affiliations of individuals or groups requesting their use.

Adopted June 18, 1948.
Amended February 2, 1961, June 27, 1967, and January 23, 1980, by the ALA Council.

APPENDIX D

INSTRUCTIONAL MATERIALS SELECTION POLICY

by Rollin George Douma

INSTRUCTIONAL MATERIALS SELECTION POLICY
OF THE ... PUBLIC SCHOOL DISTRICT*

This policy statement is the product of the following committee and represents the agreement of all committee members on this subject.

_____, representing Elementary Administration

_____, representing Secondary Administration

_____, representing Board of Education

_____, representing Parents in the Community

_____, representing School District Libraries

_____, representing Elementary Social Studies

_____, representing Secondary Social Studies

_____, representing Elementary Language Arts

_____, representing Secondary English

_____, representing School District Students

The committee feels this statement is a positive policy for the encouragement of a wide and wise use of instructional resources in our schools, as well as for the handling of any incidents of complaint that may arise concerning these resources.

This policy statement has been approved and adopted by the ... School District Board of Education,

_____, _____, _____.
month   day   year

---

*Used by permission of Rollin G. Douma.

191

TABLE OF CONTENTS

INTRODUCTION

The policies here set forth are officially those of the ... Public School District and are followed by all who are concerned with the selection of instructional materials. The purposes of these policies are to:

1. Provide a statement of philosophy and objectives for the guidance of those involved in the procedures for selection;
2. Clarify for the community the philosophy and procedure used in evaluating and selecting instructional materials;
3. Define the roles of those who share in the responsibility for the selection of instructional materials;
4. Set forth criteria for selection and evaluation of instructional materials;
5. Outline the techniques for the application of the criteria;
6. Provide a procedure for the consideration of objections to the use of particular materials in the educational program.

PHILOSOPHY AND OBJECTIVES OF MATERIALS SELECTION

The statement below, published by the National Council of Teachers of English, embodies the basic principles on which the ... Public School District selection policy is founded.

The right to read, like all rights guaranteed or implied within our constitutional tradition, can be used wisely or foolishly. In many ways, education is an effort to improve the quality of choices open to man. But to deny the freedom of choice in fear that it may be unwisely used is to destroy the freedom itself. For this reason, we respect the rights of individuals to be selective in their own reading. But for the same reason, we oppose efforts of individuals or groups to limit the freedom of choice of others or to impose their own standards or tastes upon the community at large.

The right of any individual not just to read but to read whatever he wants to read is basic to a democratic society. This right is based on an assumption that the educated and reading man can be trusted with the determination of his own actions. In effect, the reading man is freed from the bonds of discovering all things and all facts and all truths through his own direct experience, for his reading allows him to meet people, debate philosophies, and experience events far beyond the narrow confines of his own existence.

In selecting books for reading by young people ... teachers consider the contribution which each work may make to the education of the reader, its aesthetic value, its honesty, its readability for a particular group of students, and its appeal to adolescents....

* * *

What a young reader gets from any book depends both on the selection and on the reader himself. A teacher should choose books with an awareness of the student's interests, his reading ability, his mental and emotional maturity, and the values he may derive from the reading. A wide knowledge of many works, common sense, and professional dedication to students and to literature will guide the teacher in making his selections. The community that entrusts students to the care of [a] ... teacher should also trust that teacher to exercise professional judgment in selecting or recommending books. [1]

In addition, the ... Public School District affirms that the school library is primarily an educational function designed to promote the intellectual, cultural, social, and ethical development of students and to provide materials which extend and deepen the experiences encompassed in the curriculum. The ... Public School District, moreover, affirms the sharing of the responsibilities of school libraries presented in the School Library Bill of Rights for School Library Media Programs of the American Association of School Librarians:

To provide a comprehensive collection of instructional materials selected in compliance with basic, written selection principles, and to provide maximum accessibility to these materials.

To provide materials that will support the curriculum, taking into consideration the individual's needs, and the varied interests, abilities, socio-economic backgrounds, and maturity levels of the students served.

To provide materials for teachers and students that will encourage growth in knowledge, and that will develop literary, cultural and aesthetic appreciation, and ethical standards.

To provide materials which reflect the ideas and beliefs of religious, social, political, historical, and ethnic groups and their contributions to the American and world heritage and culture, thereby enabling students to develop an intellectual integrity in forming judgments.

To provide a written statement, approved by the local Boards of Education, of the procedures for meeting the challenge of censorship of materials in school library media centers.

To provide qualified professional personnel to serve teachers and students. [2]

LEGAL AUTHORITY FOR SELECTION

Chapter 26, section 882 of Michigan General School Laws states: "The board of each district shall select and approve the textbooks to be used by the pupils of the schools of its district on the subjects taught therein."

Chapter 27, section 908 of <u>Michigan General School Laws</u> states: "The board of any school district in which a library may be established in accordance with the provisions of this act shall have charge of such library and shall provide the necessary conveniences for the proper care of such library and said board shall be responsible for and shall use all moneys raised or apportioned for its support in accordance with the provisions of law...."

The board of education of the ... Public School District is therefore legally responsible for the selection and approval of books and other instructional materials in its school libraries and classrooms.

DELEGATION OF AUTHORITY FOR SELECTION

Since the board of education is a policy-making body, it delegates to the professional personnel of the school district the authority for the selection of instructional materials.

In library materials selection, responsibility for selection and acquisition is delegated to the librarians and teachers, who carry out the practices in accordance with this selection policy.

The selection of required texts for a subject is determined cooperatively by the staff members of the department or school concerned. Optional, suggested, or outside reading called for by individual teachers is left to the careful and considered judgment of the teacher of the class concerned.

In addition, each school may provide a selection of reading materials for sale to students, and each school may provide facilities for special orders by students. Responsibility for the operation of such sales shall be placed within ....

REFERENCE AIDS USED IN THE SELECTION
OF INSTRUCTIONAL MATERIALS

Reputable, unbiased, professionally prepared selection
aids shall be consulted as guides when applicable. These
may include, but are not restricted to, such sources as the
following:

1. Standard Catalog for High School Libraries
2. A Basic Book Collection for Junior High
   Schools
3. A Basic Book Collection for High Schools
4. Library Journal
5. English Journal
6. Elementary English
7. Book lists issued by the following organiza-
   tions--
   National Council of Teachers of English
   National Council of Teachers of Mathematics
   National Council for the Social Studies
   National Science Teachers Association
   Scholastic Magazines, Inc.

It is to be emphasized that selection, especially of
timely or current interest materials, should not be limited
to only a few sources. To proceed thus is to invite a delay
in acquiring what is often needed as the most up-to-date information or publication.

CRITERIA USED IN THE SELECTION OF MATERIALS

General Criteria

Materials shall be selected (1) to fill the needs of the
individual school curriculum, based on the knowledge of administrators and faculty, and (2) to fill the needs of the individual student, based on the knowledge of administrators,
faculty, parents, and students.

Truth--encompassing factual accuracy, authority, integrity, and balance--shall be a basic requirement in the
selection of informational materials. Art--encompassing

qualities of imagination, creativeness, style appropriate to
the idea, stimulating presentation, vitality, and distinction
of format--is an important factor in the selection of books
of fiction, and of nonfiction as well.

In all cases, choice of materials will be made with
the idea of inclusion of the best available rather than exclu-
sion for fear of pressure from an individual or group.
The ... Public School District agrees with the National
Council of Teachers of English that "the value and impact
of any literary work must be examined as a whole and not
in part--the impact of the entire work being more important
than the words, phrases, or incidents out of which it is
made. "³

Provision will be made, then, for a wide range of
materials on all levels of difficulty, with a diversity of appeal, and presentation of varied points of view, with the final decision for selection resting upon whether life is presented in its true proportion, whether circumstances are
realistically dealt with, and whether the material is of literary value.

Specific Criteria

Fiction is selected to meet the needs of students
varying in reading ability, social background, and taste.
Fiction is selected not only to represent literary merit but
also to provide books that are competent and successful in
all categories of fiction and to provide enjoyable experiences
for readers of all ability levels.   Although it is impossible
to set up a single standard of literary excellence, it is the
policy to select fiction which is well written and based on
authentic human experience, and to exclude fiction which is
incompetent, cheaply sentimental, intentionally sensational or
morbid or erotic, and false in its representation of human
experience.

Periodicals, newspapers, and pamphlets shall be
selected on the basis of presenting factual information,
matter of timely or current interest, divergent points of
view, value in reference, and accessibility of contents
through indexing.

Propaganda pamphlets are expected to be one-sided,
but only those whose publishers' names and statements of purpose are clearly indicated will be selected.

Film and filmstrip selection follows the general policies and objectives outlined for all other instructional materials. Film content, subject matter, and treatment are evaluated in relation to their validity, lasting value or timely importance, imagination, and originality. Criteria for selection of filmstrips include content, quality of the visual material, accuracy, and clarity of accompanying script or recording, importance of the subject in relation to curricular needs, and the unique contribution of this medium in conveying subject matter.

Recordings, musical and nonmusical, in literary and nonliterary fields, are selected by the same general principles applied to the selection of other instructional materials, plus consideration of the value of sound in conveying the subject matter.

Materials obtainable without charge should be free from excessive amounts of advertising, distortion of fact or misleading statements, with the exception of propaganda material as noted earlier. In addition, gifts are accepted on the same general principles applying to the selection of other instructional materials.

Criteria Concerning Subjects of Frequent Controversy

In the selection of materials on religious and quasi-religious subjects, preference is given to the work of informed, well-established authors whose views may be of concern to the students using the material, no matter how unconventional or contrary to tradition these views may be. Works which tend to foster hatred or intolerance toward racial groups, cults, religious organizations, or religious leaders are subject to very careful scrutiny and are selected only if the works in question have convincing curricular value.

The selection of materials which deal with controversial problems and issues or provide basic factual information on any ideology or philosophy which exerts a strong force--either favorably or unfavorably--in government, current events, politics, education, or any other phase of life should provide as fully as practicably possible for all points of view.

Materials will not be excluded on the basis of the race, nationality, or political or religious views of the author, speaker, or creator if they meet all other requirements.

Materials which contain references to or incidents of sexual behavior, violence, or profanity are subjected to a rigorous test of merit, relevance, and value in meeting the objectives of the course for which they are selected. The maturity and experience of the students by whom the material will be used are taken into consideration. Elements of sexual incident, violence, or profanity do not, however, automatically disqualify a work. Rather, the decision is made on the basis of whether the material presents life in its true proportion, whether circumstances are realistically dealt with, and whether the material meets the objectives of the course for which it is selected.

PROCEDURES FOR HANDLING OBJECTIONS TO MATERIALS

Any objection to instructional materials, either from other faculty members or administrators or from parents or members of the community, will be handled in the following way.

I. Any objection regarding instructional materials will be directed to.... The ... and the teacher of the class in which the material is used shall then hear the objection and attempt to answer it satisfactorily through an informal discussion.

   A. Any parent who, after discussion with the ... and teacher, still indicates objection to the use of the material with his child will be told that the parent's guidance function is deeply respected and that the parent is entirely free either (1) to request the teacher to substitute an alternate assignment or (2) to request that the child be placed in another class.

   B. Any faculty member, administrator, or member of the community wishing to pursue his objection beyond the informal discussion, or any parent not satisfied with the two alternatives in I-A, will be asked to follow the formal complaint procedure described below.

II. The ... shall present the complainant with two pieces of information: (1) a copy of this instructional materials selection policy and (2) a copy of the appropriate complaint form. The complaint forms are included on pages 203-206 of this policy statement.

III. The ... will inform the complainant of the standard procedure for making a formal complaint, which consists of the following:

A. To initiate a formal complaint, the complainant shall be asked to read the materials provided and to complete in writing each part of the appropriate complaint form given him.

B. The completed complaint form is to be submitted to the ... who will present it to the appropriate evaluation committee for careful consideration. The evaluation committee is appointed by the ... in consultation with teachers and administrators and is composed of representative members of the teacher group concerned with the selection of the material in question.

C. The evaluation committee will pass judgment as to whether the challenged material conforms to the principles and objectives of materials selection set down in this policy statement.

D. When the evaluation committee has carefully considered the challenged material in the light of the complainant's objections, the complainant shall be contacted and a meeting arranged by the committee chairman between the evaluation committee and the complainant at a time which is agreeable to both parties.

E. The evaluation committee reserves the right (1) to limit the number of persons presenting a complaint at this meeting to two individuals, (2) to require that separate complaint forms be completed for each challenged material, and (3) to limit the discussion that takes place in the meeting between the evaluation committee and the complainant to only those objections which have been specifically cited in the complaint form.

F. The format for the meeting shall consist of the following:

1. The chairman of the evaluation committee
shall read aloud the complaint as it was presented, and either he or a member of the
committee shall relate the findings that they
have made regarding the specific objections
cited in the complaint form.

2. The complainant shall have an opportunity to
discuss and ask questions about the findings
of the committee, clarify his own objection,
and present evidence to rebut the position
taken by the committee.

3. When the chairman of the evaluation committee has felt that the issues being dealt with
are clearly enough understood, he shall ad-
journ the meeting.

G. The evaluation committee shall reevaluate its findings in the light of the meeting and render a decision regarding the use of the challenged material
in the curriculum.

H. The decision of the evaluation committee will be
final, and the material in question will be retained
or removed according to their decision.

IV. A report of the findings and decision of the evaluation
committee shall be made to the....

V. The ..., in turn, shall inform in writing the board of
education, the superintendent, and the complainant of the decision.

REQUEST FOR RECONSIDERATION OF A BOOK

The spaces provided for answers on this form are not intended to limit comment. Please feel free to write on the back or attach additional sheets. Each portion of this form must be completed before the evaluation committee can reconsider the book.

Author _____

Title _____

Request initiated by _____

Address _____ Telephone _____

City _____ Zip code _____

Complainant represents

_____ himself

_____ name of organization _____

_____ identify other group _____

1. To what in the book do you object? Please be specific; cite pages.

2. What of value is there in this book?

3. What do you feel might be the result of reading this book?

4. Did you read the entire book? _____ What pages or sections? _____

5. Are you aware of the teacher's purpose in using this book?

6. What do you believe is the theme or purpose of this book?

7. What would you prefer the school to do about this book?

_____ do not assign or recommend it to my child

_____ withdraw it from all students

_____ send it back to the evaluation committee for reconsideration

8. In its place, what book of equal value would you recommend that would convey as valuable a picture and perspective of a society or a set of values?

_____
(Signature)

REQUEST FOR RECONSIDERATION OF
OTHER PRINTED MATERIALS

The spaces provided for answers on this form are not intended to limit comment. Please feel free to write on the back or attach additional sheets. Each portion of this form must be completed before the evaluation committee can reconsider the printed material.

Author _____ Type of material _____

Title _____

Request initiated by _____

Address _____ Telephone _____

City _____ Zip code _____

Complainant represents

_____ himself

_____ name of organization _____

_____ identify other group _____

1. To what in the printed material do you object? Please be specific: cite pages.

2. What of value is there in this printed material?

3. What do you feel might be the result of reading this material?

4. Did you read the entire work? _____ What pages or parts? _____

5. Are you aware of the teacher's purpose in using this work?

6. What do you believe is the theme or purpose of this work?

7. What would you prefer the school do about this work?

_____ do not assign or recommend it to my child

_____ withdraw it from all students

_____ send it back to the evaluation committee for reconsideration

8. In its place, what work of equal value would you recommend that would serve as well the purpose for which it was selected?

_____
(Signature)

REQUEST FOR RECONSIDERATION OF
AN AUDIO-VISUAL RESOURCE

The spaces provided for answers on this form are not intended to limit comment. Please feel free to write on the back or attach additional sheets. Each portion of this form must be completed before the evaluation committee can consider the audio-visual resource.

Author or producer_____

Type of material _____ Title _____

Request initiated by_____

Address _____ Telephone _____

City_____ Zip code _____

Complainant represents

_____himself

_____name of organization_____

_____identify other group_____

1. To what in the A-V material do you object? Please be specific.

2. What of value is there in this A-V material?

3. What do you feel might be the result of viewing or hearing this A-V material?

4. Did you view or hear the entire A-V material? _____What parts?
_____

5. Are you aware of the teacher's purpose in using this A-V?

6. What do you believe is the theme or purpose of this work?

7. What would you prefer the school do about this work?

_____do not assign or recommend it to my child

_____withdraw it from all students

_____send it back to the evaluation committee for reconsideration

8. In its place, what work of equal value would you recommend that would serve as well the purpose for which it was selected?

_____
(Signature)

REQUEST FOR RECONSIDERATION OF A SPEAKER

The spaces provided for answers on this form are not intended to limit comment. Please feel free to write on the back or attach additional sheets. Each portion of this form must be completed before the evaluation committee can reconsider the presentation.

Speaker_____ Occasion_____

Topic of presentation_____

Request initiated by_____

Address_____ Telephone_____

City_____ Zip code_____

Complainant represents

_____ himself

_____ name of organization_____

_____ identify other group_____

1. To what in the presentation do you object? Please be specific.

2. What of value is there in this presentation?

3. What do you feel might be the result of hearing this presentation?

4. Did you hear the entire presentation?_____ What parts?

5. Are you aware of the purpose in presenting this speaker?

6. What do you believe is the theme or purpose of this presentation?

7. What would you prefer the school do about this presentation?

_____ do not assign or recommend it to my child

_____ do not assign or recommend it to any student

_____ have the evaluation committee reconsider it

8. In his place, what speaker of equal value would you recommend who would serve as well the purpose for which he was selected?

_____
(Signature)

FOOTNOTES

[1]Kenneth L. Donelson, ed., The Students' Right to Read (Urbana, Ill.: National Council of Teachers of English, 1972), pp. 7-9.

[2]American Association of School Librarians, School Library Bill of Rights for School Library Media Programs (Chicago: American Library Association, approved by American Association of School Librarians Board of Directors, June, 1969).

[3]Donelson, The Students' Right to Read, p. 8.

INDEX

218 / Index

school library media centers   43, 66, 73, 81, 99, 126, 164,
    165
School Research Information Service (SRIS)   96
security   68, 79, 125, 153, 170
selection   22, 115
    criteria for   86, 89-94, 104, 116
    policy   29, 85-86
    poor examples of   90, 155
    see also gifts; free materials; censorship
selection centers   12
    see also evaluation centers
service   22, 23
    functions   151-152
    policies   27
    to students and faculty   4-6
    to teachers   6-10
    see also types (e. g., circulation, reference)
shelf reading   36, 49
shelving   125, 163
    equipment   72, 73
    standards   72
    weight limits   70
    see also collections--maintenance and organization
signs   81-83
slides   51, 53, 98, 133, 157
    equipment for   53, 57
SMERC   8, 121
sound control   70, 72, 79
space   29
    checklist   73
    production requirements   57-59, 73
    standards   66-67
    see also study space
space planning   see architectural planning
special collections departments   11, 32, 89
SRIS   see School Research Information Center
staff   see support staff; professional staff; student aides
standardized tests   see tests, standardized
standards   see National Association of State Directors of
        Teacher Education Certification; National Council for
        the Accreditation of Teacher Education (NCATE)
standards for media programs   35-36, 66-67
state adopted materials   12, 103-105, 161
    adding notation for   125, 127, 138-139, 140
    see also textbooks; evaluation centers; censorship
state education departments   3, 8, 12, 28, 33, 41, 44, 48,
        101, 104, 114, 179